STRAIGHT TALK ABOUT
SOCIAL SECURITY

Robert M. Ball
with Thomas N. Bethell

Straight Talk
about Social
Security

An Analysis
of the Issues
in the
Current Debate

A Century Foundation/Twentieth Century Fund Report

1998 • The Century Foundation Press • New York

The Century Foundation/Twentieth Century Fund sponsors and supervises timely analyses of economic policy, foreign affairs, and domestic political issues. Not-for-profit and nonpartisan, the Fund was founded in 1919 and endowed by Edward A. Filene.

Cataloging-in-Publication Data

Ball, Robert M.
Straight talk about social security: an analysis of the issues in the current debate / Robert M. Ball with Thomas N. Bethell.
    p. cm
"A Century Foundation report."
Includes bibliographical references and index.
ISBN 0-87078-422-6
    1. Social security--United States.   2. Social security--United States--Finance.
    I. Bethell, Thomas N.   II. Title.
HD7125.B279   1998   98–22807
368.4'3'00973--dc21   CIP

Cover design and illustration: Claude Goodwin
Manufactured in the United States of America.

FOREWORD

Americans have an apparently insatiable appetite for things that go bump in the night. It's no accident that Stephen King and *Friday the 13th* attract readers and audiences year in and year out. Even policy wonks, it seems, can't resist the attention that comes from telling a good scare story. The current favorite involves the dire consequences of the aging of the baby boom generation.

Sometime in the not too distant future, we are told, the good life will all but cease, crushed under the weight of the pension and health care needs of the boomers. Social Security, the nation's premier social insurance program, even faces "bankruptcy." We are told that, without sweeping changes, the program cannot be expected to continue payments to retirees in the next century. Yet, paradoxically, we are also told that, if nothing changes, future workers will be heavily burdened with higher and higher payroll taxes. Never mind the inconsistency between these two versions of tomorrow. (If it won't be going to retirees, why would the taxes keep increasing?) The point being driven home is consistent: failure to shrink or replace Social Security will lead to certain disaster.

Two events seem to have triggered the current intense debate about the future of Social Security: first, the fact that the oldest boomers hit 50 last year, and second, a number of the recommendations in the report of the Advisory Council on Social Security published in 1997. The council based its opinions on the forecasts of the Board of Trustees of the Federal Old-Age and Survivors Insurance and Disability Insurance Trust Funds, which looks 75 years into the future to determine whether, according to the best demographic and economic forecasts available, Social Security will have enough money to continue to pay benefits to those in retirement. In many ways, the council did an admirable job, but they could not reach a consensus on the most desirable changes in the program. In any event, no group could have accommodated all the sharply differing views about both Social Security's prospects and the proper policies to deal with it.

In this atmosphere of confounded facts and alarmist rhetoric, the need for factual and clear reporting has been especially acute. Therefore, The Century Foundation/Twentieth Century Fund has been attempting to provide a solid base of information for citizens of all ages. Over the last three years, we have published a number of works looking at this program and other issues related to it. Our Basics pamphlet series includes volumes on *Social Security Reform* (2nd edition, 1998), *Medicare Reform*, and *Medicaid Reform,* and Robert Eisner has prepared two reports for us—*The Great Deficit Scares: The Federal Deficit, Trade, and Social Security* and *Social Security: More, Not Less.* In addition, this year we will launch our Social Security Network on-line, and publish a number of white papers and books relating to Social Security, pensions, and the aging of America.

Still, in the early spring of 1998, the need for current facts and informed analysis seemed greater than ever. Therefore, we are especially pleased that Robert Ball, former commissioner of Social Security and a member of the recent Advisory Council on Social Security, has prepared, with Thomas N. Bethell, the following closely reasoned and important report on the central issues in the current debate about the program. Ball's reflections on the key issues and his agenda for reform should be required reading for all Americans.

On behalf of the Trustees of The Century Foundation, I thank him for his work on this publication and his leadership in the field of social insurance.

RICHARD C. LEONE, *PRESIDENT*
The Twentieth Century Fund
April 1998

CONTENTS

TABLES AND FIGURE

1

MISUNDERSTANDINGS ABOUT THE FINANCING OF SOCIAL SECURITY

M uch of the public concern about the future of Social Security stems from widespread misinformation about the financing of the present system—misinformation reported so often that it has become part of the conventional wisdom. More than anything else, this accounts for the growing lack of confidence in the system, particularly among younger Americans. The pervasiveness of this misinformation is going to make it difficult to develop a sensible policy aimed at restoring long-term Social Security balance, and, among other things, argues for a stepped-up effort to communicate the facts about Social Security financing prior to any legislative effort.

Four major areas of confusion need to be addressed:

♦ the meaning of trust fund[1] exhaustion;

♦ the significance of the declining number of workers per retiree;

♦ the impact of Social Security on the federal budget; and

♦ Social Security as an entitlement.

THE MEANING OF TRUST FUND EXHAUSTION

When the Social Security trustees report that the Social Security trust fund will be exhausted in about 2030, as they have each year for the past several years, many journalists and other commentators take this to mean that from 2030 on there will be no money to pay benefits. This is not the case.

Under present law, income from trust fund investments plays a relatively small part in financing benefit payments. Most of the financing comes directly from Social Security taxes on employers and employees, and this source of support is ongoing. The income from the Social Security tax rates now being charged would be sufficient to fund three-fourths of Social Security's expenses for decades after 2030—even with those expenses increasing—and would still meet two-thirds of the cost 75 years from now.

In other words, Social Security is not "going broke." Far from it. What the system will be facing in 2030 (in the absence of corrective steps in the meantime) is a shortfall. This problem should be addressed sooner rather than later. The point, however, is that we are not starting from scratch after 2030; the major part of benefit costs is already financed.

THE SIGNIFICANCE OF THE DECLINING NUMBER OF WORKERS PER RETIREE

Another point about Social Security financing that is broadly misunderstood concerns the declining ratio of workers (those paying in) to the number of beneficiaries (those taking out).

In starting up a new contributory retirement system in which eligibility for benefits depends upon contributions and work in covered employment, no one is eligible at first because no one has worked in covered employment or paid contributions. Most of those who are elderly have stopped working and will never be eligible for benefits, so the proportion of the elderly receiving benefits goes up slowly and only as younger workers who have worked within the system reach retirement age. Although contributions to Social Security started in

1937, as late as 1950 only 21 percent of the elderly were eligible for benefits.

On the other hand, those working under the system were contributing regardless of age, with the result that in the mid-1940s there were 42 contributing workers per beneficiary. By 1950 the ratio had dropped to 16 workers per beneficiary, while today the ratio is approaching 3 to 1, and eventually will drop to about 2 to 1. The inevitability of the decline from 42:1 to 16:1 to 3:1 or so, has long been evident and has been anticipated in financing the program. But this fact is often misunderstood by commentators, who treat the changing ratio of workers to beneficiaries as if it were a recently discovered phenomenon that throws the future financing of Social Security into doubt.[2]

Confusion about the meaning of a declining worker/beneficiary ratio in Social Security is linked to confusion about the trend in the even more fundamental ratio of workers to non-workers of all ages whose support must come from the total volume of goods and services that workers produce. Are workers in the future faced with the dismal prospect of carrying the burden of support for more and more non-workers? That is the impression created by depictions of baby boomer retirement, beginning about 2010, as a back-breaking load for workers. But this is not the whole story.

It is true that the ratio of those age 65 and older to those aged 20-64 will climb rapidly once the babyboomers enter old age, going from 0.214 in 2010 to an estimated 0.370 for 2035 and to somewhat over 0.400 in 2065. But what is left out of this picture is that the trend within the other big group of non-workers—children—has been going the other way, and the combined ratio of *all* dependents to workers is not expected to be as high again at any time in the entire 75 years of Social Security forecasting as it was, for example, in the decade from 1960 to 1970. At that time the ratio averaged over 0.900—in other words, very close to one non-worker per worker—while in 1995 it was only 0.710. Looking ahead, even with the increases in the number and longevity of the elderly, the ratio as projected will not reach 0.800 until 2055 and will not reach 0.830 until 2075. The basic economic point is unmistakable: The picture of future workers staggering under an increasing and intolerable load of dependents is inaccurate. Relative to those of working age, there will be more elderly but fewer children.[3]

SOCIAL SECURITY AND THE FEDERAL BUDGET

It has also become part of conventional wisdom that Social Security has been a major cause of federal budget deficits. This is not so. Since 1937, when Social Security taxes were first collected, Social Security has taken in approximately $5.5 trillion and paid out approximately $4.9 trillion, leaving a balance of about $600 billion in a contingency reserve. Clearly that doesn't add to the deficit. In fact, speaking in terms of the "unified budget"—as budget negotiators do in spite of the fact that the law has put Social Security off-budget—Social Security has been a major contributor to reaching a balanced budget. Under present law, Social Security income is expected to exceed expenditures by $80 billion in 1997, by $92 billion in 2000, and by $130 billion in 2006. Without Social Security, the government would have to find these additional amounts elsewhere in order to be able to present the same budget balances for these years.

SOCIAL SECURITY AS AN ENTITLEMENT

The false notion that Social Security has been part of the deficit problem gets expressed most forcefully in attacks on "runaway entitlements." Social Security is, of course, an "entitlement" program—and rightly so. The concept is of great importance to the future economic security of those covered by Social Security. "Entitlement," in the context of Social Security, means that all people without distinction of sex, race, or income are entitled to receive benefits in an amount specified by law once they have met the objective criteria of having worked in employment covered by the program for a specified period of time and have met other objective qualifications—for example, by reaching age 62 for reduced retirement benefits, or by having a total disability estimated to last for a long and indefinite period, or by being the widow, widower, or child of an insured worker.

"Entitlement" means that Congress has set the conditions of eligibility in law, and the administrators of the system have no discretion beyond evaluating the proof of whether an applicant meets those conditions. If an applicant for Social Security benefits feels that eligibility has been wrongfully denied or that the amount of the benefit has been incorrectly computed, he or she can, after an administrative hearing, appeal to the federal courts all the way to the Supreme Court. Social Security is very explicitly an entitlement—and it is a good thing that it is. We need to rehabilitate the term "entitlement."

The opposite of an entitlement is a discretionary payment, which if applied to Social Security could mean—as it does in some programs—that eligibility conditions and benefit levels would be determined not by long-term considerations but by the exigencies of short-term budget cycles in which various programs compete against one another for funding. For Social Security, with its uniquely long-term commitments, this approach would clearly be unworkable. Social Security should, of course, be subject to periodic review and its value assessed, just as with other programs, but not as part of the annual budget cycle.

In the case of Social Security and Medicare, as distinct from certain other entitlement programs such as food stamps, there is not only a legal entitlement but also, since the benefits grow out of past earnings and contributions, the benefits are looked upon as an earned entitlement. Thus, although the Supreme Court has ruled that benefits and conditions for payment may be changed by law if the changes affect a broad category of participants in ways that are reasonable and nondiscriminatory, there is considerable reluctance on the part of lawmakers to substantially reduce protection or make any radical changes. There is good reason for this. Social Security commitments are, as noted, very long-term. People are contributing now toward benefits that may not be due for some 40 years in the future, and a high degree of stability in both contribution rates and benefit levels is a valued part of the Social Security tradition.

2

RESTORING SOCIAL SECURITY TO LONG-TERM BALANCE: WHAT SHOULD BE DONE?

As has been the pattern for the past several years, the Social Security Trustees in their 1997 report, looking ahead for 75 years, anticipate a long-term deficit, which they estimate at an average of 2.23 percent of payroll.[1] If we act promptly, we can substantially reduce this projected deficit without having to make major tax increases or benefit cuts and without sacrificing or compromising the basic principles and traditional advantages of the program. There is no need to turn to a system of individual accounts (discussed in Chapter 4), which in themselves do nothing to help the long-range balance of Social Security. A large part of the job of restoring the program to long-term balance can be done by making several relatively minor changes.

MINOR CHANGES SIMILAR TO THOSE MADE IN THE PAST

To begin with, the options available include several that are entirely within the tradition of the present Social Security program:

- extending coverage in order to make the program truly universal;

- increasing taxation of benefits in line with taxation of other defined-benefit contributory plans;

- improving the accuracy of cost-of-living adjustments in accordance with anticipated changes to the Consumer Price Index;

- moderately increasing future taxes; and

- moderately reducing future benefits.

The first three of these changes would be desirable in any case from an equity standpoint. Whether or not all of them are politically feasible right now is a matter for discussion.

1. MAKE THE PROGRAM TRULY UNIVERSAL

Over time, almost all occupational groups have been incorporated into the Social Security program, and coverage is now nearly universal, including most full-time state and local government employees. But about 25 percent of these state and local employees are not covered. This is the last large group of excluded workers. Phasing them into the program would be beneficial to Social Security's financing largely because, as with other groups when newly covered, revenues accrue for many years before benefits must be paid out. The effect of this change is to reduce the long-term 2.23 percent-of-payroll deficit by about 10 percent or 0.25 percent of payroll.

It would be advantageous to these workers and their families to be part of the universal system while retaining supplementary protection under their own plans. They would have greater freedom to change jobs without forfeiting protection; improved protection against inflation; better survivor and disability protection in most cases; and reliable coverage for spouses (which is not required under some state and local government pension plans). And in any case, it is only fair for all state and local employees to be contributing to the nation's social insurance system, which protects them as taxpayers against what could otherwise be the very substantial tax burden of supporting much larger welfare and relief programs.

The best approach would be to phase in Social Security coverage by covering only new hires, as was done when coverage was extended to federal employees. This gives the employing entity time to adapt to any increases in cost, and if provision is made for implementing this change a year or two after enactment, there will also be time to work out the integration of Social Security with state and local retirement systems in order to ensure that employees have optimal protection. There will be opposition in particular states, but it should be possible to get agreement for this change.

2. INCREASE THE TAXATION OF BENEFITS

It is reasonable to ask present beneficiaries to help bring Social Security into long-term balance, as long as the burden is fairly distributed. The most equitable way to do this is to apply the progressive income tax rules to Social Security benefits in the same way they apply to other contributory defined-benefit plans, so that Social Security benefits are taxed to the extent that they exceed what the worker paid in. This change would reduce the projected long-term deficit by about 0.13 percent of payroll.

In connection with this change, as a matter of fairness Social Security beneficiaries should not be given the special exemption from income taxes that they now have solely because of being beneficiaries, whereas other people with the same level of income are taxed. Accordingly, the current exemption for beneficiaries with annual incomes below $25,000 for single persons and $32,000 for couples should be repealed. Beneficiaries at the lower end of the income scale (about 30 percent of all beneficiaries) would be unaffected by this change because their benefits would remain untaxed under general income-tax rules protecting low-income people. This change would save Social Security another 10 percent or about 0.23 percent of payroll.[2]

3. IMPROVE THE ACCURACY OF SOCIAL SECURITY COST-OF-LIVING ADJUSTMENTS

The Bureau of Labor Statistics (BLS) is currently considering changes to the Consumer Price Index (CPI) in order to improve its accuracy in measuring inflation. There seems to be general agreement that any correction of the CPI should be reflected in Social Security Cost-of-Living Adjustments (COLA). Although occasionally the argument is made that there should be a separate CPI for the elderly, this line of reasoning is probably not a major barrier to translating a BLS reduction in the CPI into reduced COLA increases. (The 1994-96 Advisory Council agreed that it would be an unwise precedent to change the CPI measure by legislation without BLS support, believing that adjustment should be based on technical considerations rather than introduce political competition, as would inevitably accompany any effort to change the CPI by legislation in the absence of a BLS recommendation.)

It is now reasonable to anticipate a downward adjustment in the expected CPI growth rate of 0.20 percentage points as a result of BLS's stated intent to correct the "lower level substitution bias" by 1999. BLS now proposes to substitute a geometric weighting in the formula for the present arithmetic weighting in a major proportion of the some 9,000 categories in the CPI market basket. Additional reduction would result if the market basket were brought up to date more often than the present 10-year timetable. If done every year, which seems reasonable given the importance of this measure, the reduction would be another 0.10 percentage point or so. For the purpose of these cost estimates, the assumption is that there will be a total reduction of 0.30 percentage points in the CPI—0.20 percentage points from the introduction of geometric weighting and 0.10 from updating the market basket annually. This results in reducing the long-range deficit by nearly 19 percent, or 0.42 percent of payroll.

The combined effect of these three changes that improve the equity and accuracy of the system is to reduce the projected deficit from 2.23 percent of payroll to 1.34 percent. Small increases in taxes and cuts in benefits reduce the deficit further.

4. INCREASE THE MAXIMUM EARNINGS BASE

At one time, the maximum earnings base—the level of annual earnings above which earnings are neither taxed nor credited for the purpose of computing benefits—covered 90 percent of all wages in covered employment. Today, however, the base ($68,400 in 1998) is covering a smaller and smaller proportion of earnings; this is a result of the fact that wages are increasing faster for the higher-paid than for others. By 2006 the base is expected to cover only 84.5 percent of earnings. Under present law, the base is scheduled to increase automatically each year with increases in average wages. It would take an additional 4 percent each year between the years 2000 and 2009 in order to bring the proportion of earnings covered back up to 90 percent. But with the base now considerably below that target, increases of the magnitude necessary to entirely close the gap may be ill-advised. Higher-income earners would be required to contribute substantially more but without being able to expect anything like a commensurate increase in benefits. Accordingly, I would propose closing only half of the gap—that is, going from 84.5 to 87.3 percent over 10 years—by increasing the maximum earnings base 2 percent each year above the automatic increase. The effect in any given year would ordinarily be modest as compared to the automatic increase taking place anyway. This change reduces the projected long-term deficit by about 0.27 percent of payroll.

5. Increase the Length of the Averaging Period

The wage averaging period, which for decades now has started for almost all workers with 1951, has been gradually increasing as wages have been posted for more and more years. In 1991, wages were being posted for 40 years and, as has always been the case when averaging, retired workers were allowed to drop the five years of lowest earnings, resulting in 1991 in basing benefits on the average of the highest 35 years. This is the maximum number required in the basic law, so the averaging period has remained at 35 years since 1991. Setting the basic limit at 35 years is entirely arbitrary. The objective is to relate the benefit to the worker's career earnings, indexed to the present and with some leeway for periods of illness, unemployment, or special family obligations. With additional years of earnings since 1991, it is now feasible to relate the benefit to a some-what longer career average while maintaining the five-year forgiveness period. Since most people work more than 35 years, counting more years would cause benefits to reflect average career earnings more accurately than they now do. But lengthening the averaging period also lowers benefits because earnings for currently excluded years are necessarily lower than the 35 highest years now used in computing benefits. Doing so reduces benefits somewhat for those with fewer years under the program and those who have less than full-year earnings. Raising the end point to 38 years would reduce benefits an average of 3 percent and reduce the Social Security deficit by 0.27 percent of payroll. The comparable figures for 39 and 40 years are 4 percent and 0.48 percent and 5 percent and 0.59, respectively (without adjusting for interaction with any other changes).

A good case can be made for this method of trimming benefits, but the proposal does arouse controversy. It reduces benefits somewhat more for workers with intermittent rather than steady wage records. Since women are more likely than men to go in and out of the workforce, the argument is made that this proposal is disadvantageous to more women than men. This is true to a limited extent, but because of Social Security's weighted benefit formula, which favors those with intermittent wage records, and because of the continuance of the five-year forgiveness period, workers going in and out of the workforce would continue to receive very favorable treatment. The issue is whether to favor the intermittent worker slightly less than under present law.

The net effect of these five proposals, as shown in Table 2.1, is to reduce the projected long-term deficit from 2.23 percent of payroll to 0.72 percent.

This brings the deficit well within the customary definition of "close actuarial balance"—that is, with expenditures within 5 percent of income over the long run—and postpones the estimated date of trust fund exhaustion by more than 20 years, pushing it back from 2030 to beyond 2050.

One could argue that this would be enough for a first step toward long-term balance, and that additional options could then be explored over the next few years. After all, the 1977 amendments aimed at achieving a 50-year rather than a 75-year balance, and 50 years is a long time indeed compared to the much shorter periods over which other nations view their social insurance systems. I would prefer, however, to recommend changes now that will eliminate the entire 75-year deficit.

This could be done by providing for a modest increase in the contribution rate and a modest reduction in replacement rates beyond

TABLE 2.1
Restoring Social Security to Long-term Balance: An Initial Package of Options to Reduce the Deficit*

Proposal	Comment	Reduces Deficit
1. Make the program universal, gradually extending coverage to all full-time state and local government workers by covering workers hired after 2000.	Most state and local government workers are already covered by Social Security. The 3.7 million who are not are the last major group in the labor force not covered.	-0.25
2. Increase the taxation of benefits and drop the special income tax exemption that applies only to Social Security beneficiaries.	Benefits should be taxed to the extent they exceed what the worker has paid in, as in other contributory defined-benefit plans, and dropping the special exemption would improve income tax equity (the lowest income beneficiaries, about 30% of the total, would still be untaxed).	-0.36
3. Change the Social Security cost-of-living adjustment (COLA) to reflect corrections to the Consumer Price Index (CPI).	With the CPI presently believed to overstate inflation, changes contemplated by BLS plus annual pricing of the market basket should result in a more accurate CPI and smaller COLAs.	-0.42
4. Increase the maximum earnings base an additional 2% each year during the 2000–2009 period.	At one time 90% of wages in covered employment were under the base, above which earnings are neither taxed nor credited for benefit computation purposes. The base will soon cover only 84.5% of wages; this change moves halfway back to the 90% standard, increasing coverage to 87.3%.	-0.27
5. Increase the length of the wage-averaging period for benefit computation purposes from 35 to 38 years.	Current 35-year averaging period is arbitrary. As the longevity of the program increases, it is feasible to extend the averaging period. Increasing it from 35 to 38 years, and thus more closely relating benefits to the worker's career-long earnings, reduces benefits for those becoming eligible in the future by 3% on average.	-0.27
Balance after implementing above changes (*adjusted for interaction of proposals*):		-0.72%

*Assumes an average long-term (75-year) deficit of 2.23% of payroll as estimated by the Social Security Trustees.

the benefit cut that results from lengthening the averaging period and increasing the taxation of benefits.

6. INCREASE THE CONTRIBUTION RATE

Increasing the contribution rate by 0.20 percentage points for workers, matched by employers, assures that wage-earners will be making at least a modest contribution to closing the long-range deficit. This proposal would increase what they pay by $20 per $10,000 of annual earnings (see Table 2.2). This change would reduce the remaining long-term deficit by 0.37 percent of payroll—leaving 0.35 percent of payroll to be met by a benefit cut. Since the benefits payable in the future under present law are not by any means too high, benefit cuts beyond those resulting from the suggested increase in the tax on benefits and the lengthening of the averaging period, as discussed above, are undesirable, but modifying the benefit formula to produce a moderate cut should be considered if other options, discussed later, are rejected.

TABLE 2.2
RESTORING SOCIAL SECURITY TO LONG-TERM BALANCE:
PACKAGE 2 OF OPTIONS TO CONSIDER
(In combination with the first five proposals summarized in Table 2.1)

Option	Comment	Reduces Deficit
6. Increase the contribution rate by 0.20 percentage points.	Amounts to deducting $20 per $10,000 of annual earnings.	-0.37
7. Reduce benefits by modifying the benefit formula gradually so as to maintain 1997 real benefit levels but cut replacement rates 5% by 2029.	Assumes that future beneficiaries should share in sacrifices needed to reach long-term balance. Reduces replacement rates but ensures that beneficiaries in the future get at least the benefit amounts going currently to new beneficiaries.	-0.35
Balance after implementing above changes (*adjusted for interaction of proposals*):		-0.04%

7. MODIFY THE PRESENT BENEFIT FORMULA

An additional way to reduce benefits is to change the benefit formula. This can be done, of course, without changing the relative positions of intermittent and steady workers or the positions of the low-paid. On the other hand, when such a change is made the positions of low-paid and intermittent workers could be improved at the expense of the higher-paid.

Since the formula is already skewed substantially in favor of those who are worse off, I would urge that any cuts from a benefit-formula change be evenhanded across the range of covered wages. It is important to retain the support of higher-paid workers for Social Security, and it is a matter of delicate balance to determine just how far it is wise to go in pursuing income redistribution through this program. It seems to me that we now have it about right.

If a benefit cut is deemed necessary, it should not affect those already retired, and should be phased in so that the benefits for those retiring in the future are not cut below the amounts being paid to those retiring today. This can be done because, while present law maintains benefits at approximately a fixed percentage of past earnings (the replacement rate), new benefit amounts rise for future retirees as wages rise (wages are assumed to rise 0.9 percent per year faster than the CPI). If benefits are reduced, the timing should be such that future beneficiaries get lower replacement rates but not lower real benefits. This principle requires timing the reductions in the replacement rate to take into account the provision of present law that, beginning in the year 2000, gradually raises the normal retirement age from 65 to 67.

The benefit formula for 1998 is 90 percent of the first $477 of average indexed monthly earnings (AIME), 32 percent of the next $2,875 of AIME, and 15 percent for any AIME above that. A 3 percent cut in average benefits could be achieved by changes in the three factors. This cut could be made gradually beginning with beneficiaries becoming eligible in 2020 and reaching 3 percent (87.3, 31.04, and 14.55) for those becoming eligible in 2029 and later. A 5 percent reduction could be reached by changing the three factors to 85.5, 30.4, and 14.25. These cuts would save 0.21 percent of payroll for the 3 percent cut (see Table 2.2) and 0.35 percent of payroll for the 5 percent cut. Under this approach and with these effective dates, real benefits for future retirees would never be less than benefits being paid to new retirees today.

ADDITIONAL OPTIONS

There are other options—alternatives to the above proposals—that would also bring the program into long-range balance. Two in particular deserve attention here because, whatever their merit, they will certainly be considered as part of the legislative process.

8. INCREASE THE NORMAL RETIREMENT AGE BEYOND THE PROVISIONS OF CURRENT LAW

The normal retirement age (NRA), the age of first eligibility for full benefits, is now 65. Under present law it is scheduled to increase gradually to age 67 in 2022. Benefits could be reduced by providing for further increases. Accelerating the scheduled change and raising the NRA automatically as longevity increases is an approach that has attracted considerable support, and one that was endorsed by eight members of the 1994–96 Advisory Council. I am opposed to any such change, particularly in the near term, for the reasons discussed in the council report.[3] But if anything along this line is done, the least harmful approach would be to let present law stand until the NRA reaches 67 in 2022, and *then* begin indexing it to life expectancy. This would allow sufficient time before the change becomes effective to see whether in fact the present-law change to 67 is working out and whether workers both want to and are able to work later into their lives. If the necessary societal adjustments are slow in coming, the indexing timetable could be adjusted. This change would reduce the projected long-term deficit by another 14 percent or 0.30 percent of payroll.

9. APPLY THE SOCIAL SECURITY TAX ON EMPLOYERS TO THE ENTIRE PAYROLL

The amount of wages on which workers pay Social Security taxes is the same amount used for benefit credits. This is an important principle that follows from the concept of Social Security benefits making up for wage loss because of the old age, disability, or death of a family breadwinner. The principle preserves the contributory nature of the system and limits the amount of redistribution from higher-paid to lower-paid wage-earners in a way that seems reasonable to most Social Security participants. If, on the other hand, workers were required to pay on all earnings without limit, the relationship of benefits to contributions would be greatly weakened, and with this weakening would come the possibility of a very different attitude toward Social Security on the part of the higher-paid.

The tax on the employer, however, can be thought of as going to the Social Security system in general rather than being linked to each individual employee, and a case can be made that, as a tax on payrolls, it should be applied to the entire payroll. This would reduce the deficit by well over half, or 1.20 percent of payroll. (The reduction is as large as it is because there are no offsetting benefit increases, as would be the case with an increase in the maximum earnings base governing both taxes and benefit credits.)[4]

10. Invest Part of Social Security's Buildup in Stocks

Another change that would eliminate the need for either the benefit cuts or the contribution rate increases discussed above as items 6 and 7 would be to invest a portion of the Social Security trust fund in private equities. Under present law the traditionally pay-as-you-go Social Security system moves in the direction of partial advance funding with a trust fund buildup until about 2020, but then dissipates the trust fund over the following 10 years and does not rebuild it. However, various combinations of the proposals discussed above designed to bring the program into long-range balance have the effect of building the fund indefinitely into the future and explicitly shifting the system to partial advance funding. (This would substantially reduce the contribution rates needed to support the system as compared to pay-as-you-go rates; see Tables 2.4, page 26 and 2.5, page 27 later in this discussion.)

Building a fund of considerable size, as would now happen, raises sharply for the first time the issue of trust fund investment. As long as the system followed a pay-as-you-go plan, with reserves at a contingency level equal to only about one to one-and-a-half times the following year's outgo, the investment returns had little effect on long-range financing. But with the fund building because of partial advance funding, the rate of return on investment becomes important.

A policy of investing part of the fund buildup in stocks—rather than exclusively in lower-yielding long-term government bonds, as required by present law—could make a major contribution to reducing the long-term deficit and make benefit cuts or contribution-rate increases as described above unnecessary. Investing 40 percent of Social Security's accumulating funds in equities would reduce the deficit by approximately 0.92 percent of payroll. (Interaction with other proposals could reduce this effect by as much as 10 percent but would still be enough to eliminate the 0.72 deficit left after adopting universal coverage, additional taxation of benefits, taking account of BLS changes in the CPI, increasing the earnings base, and lengthening the averaging period [see Table 2.1].)

Just about all other public and private pension plans invest in stocks, and Social Security contributors should have the same advantages that are available to participants in other plans. Improving investment returns for Social Security would not only help eliminate its projected deficit but would also improve the benefit/contribution ratio for younger workers and future generations. In fact, if the problem presented for solution is not solely the elimination of the long-term deficit but also the improvement in the Social Security rate of return for young workers, there is an additional important reason for interest in direct equity investment.

The problem of the relatively low rate of return in Social Security for those now young as compared to the rate of return experienced by earlier participants in Social Security arises because, when the Social Security program began, it was decided to pay retirement benefits to the first generation of workers even though their contributions to the system fell far short of paying for their own benefits. This started the system down the road of pay-as-you-go rather than reserve financing.

It would have been possible to have had a fund buildup in addition to paying benefits from the beginning, but in practice this was never done. For decades the Social Security Act provided for future contribution-rate levels that would have done just that, giving us a system of partial-advance funding, as is now so widely advocated. (Virtually no one advocated the sacrifices that would have been necessary to produce full funding and full current payments.) But these rates were never allowed to go into effect, and the system has operated close to pay-as-you-go. Now, unless the system is changed, there is little financial help to be expected from earnings on the present Social Security fund, as there would be in the case of a system of private or, for that matter, public investment. Thus, in comparing future rates of return from a funded system and Social Security, Social Security is at a disadvantage equal, in the first instance, to what the earnings would have been on the accumulation of a full reserve.

On the other hand, our national system of Social Security has much lower administrative costs than would be the case under most of the current proposals to shift the system toward relying on individual investment accounts. The costs of managing the accounts plus the added costs (in some proposals) of converting the accumulated funds to annuities at market rates upon retirement would greatly reduce the real rates of return, to the point where they would compare very unfavorably with the rate of return from a Social Security system centrally investing in equities.

For example, under the Personal Security Accounts (PSA) plan proposed by five members of the 1994–96 Advisory Council, workers would contribute 5 percent of earnings annually to private accounts. Over 40 years, the annual cost of managing the accounts (estimated by the PSA plan's sponsors at one percent of the accumulating funds) would reduce the benefits by 20 percent or more. On top of that, the cost of converting the account balances into annuities (an option under the PSA plan rather than compulsory as in some other proposals) would reduce the benefit by another 20 percent or so—in part because of the cost of adverse selection (the risk that annuities, which guarantee an income until death, will be disproportionately purchased by those most likely to live long into retirement). Benefits under the PSA approach are thus reduced over the long term by 40 percent or more. Clearly, whatever financial advantage is obtainable by partial funding in a private accounts system is obtainable by the same degree of funding in a central Social Security system, without the administrative costs of individual accounts.

Not all of the partial privatization plans have the administrative drawbacks of the PSA plan. For example, the Individual Accounts (IA) plan proposed by 1994–96 Advisory Council chairman Edward Gramlich avoids the market costs of buying annuities by making conversion of funds to annuities compulsory and thus universal. And because the IA plan would channel individual investments into a limited number of government-managed funds, its administrative costs would be much lower than the PSA plan with its essentially unlimited choice of investment vehicles. (But the IA plan has many drawbacks of its own, as discussed in Chapter 4.)

Nevertheless it is highly desirable to improve the rate of return under Social Security for young workers and future generations who see themselves as disadvantaged as compared to recipients who came before, and as the 1994–96 Advisory Council recognized, any solutions to the long-term deficit problem requiring benefit cuts or increased contributions make future rates of return for Social Security lower. In this context, investment in equities is especially attractive. This would improve the rate of return for workers now young and for future generations, while at the same time greatly reducing the Social Security deficit.

The rate of return is, of course, only one criterion among many for determining what is the best retirement system for the long run. But even if the rate of return were given great emphasis and there was a desire to move very substantially toward a funded system for the future, there is a large transition cost that would have to be paid by the generation of workers just now beginning work and perhaps by the next one as well. Whether the accumulating funds arise through private accounts or through a change in the government plan, the transition generation(s) would have to pay twice: once to pay for the benefits of those who have accumulated rights under the present system and once for their own at least partially funded benefits.

The six of us on the Advisory Council who pressed for consideration of trust fund investment in equities developed the outline of a model[5] designed to protect the neutrality of investment policy by indexing investments to practically the entire market. The selection of indexes and portfolio managers would be under the general direction of a Federal Reserve-type board with members appointed for long and staggered terms. Portfolio managers would be selected by bid from organizations qualified by long experience with very large indexed private funds.[6]

Relying on the market for retirement income is risky for the individual—in part because the dates of investing are more or less fixed by the time of first going to work and the time of retiring. Although the individual would have the choice of moving investments between equities and bonds, investors could hardly anticipate when such shifts would be desirable except for the general pattern of emphasis on equities when young, with increasing amounts in bonds as retirement approaches. In contrast, direct investment by Social Security would be very long term, and consequently the volatility of the market would have little effect in the long run on the income from stocks held by Social Security.

Without regard to how it is invested, a sizable increase in national savings would result from shifting Social Security from pay-as-you-go to partial reserve financing. As the fund builds up so do national savings, but the key point is that growth in national savings comes principally from a shift to partial reserve financing, not from how the accumulating fund is invested.[7] In considering whether to allow Social Security investment in stocks, the most important consideration would be equity, not national savings. It is only equitable for Social Security contributors to get an equal return for what they pay in, as do contributors to other types of retirement plans, since both forms of saving make the same contribution to the broad economy. Equal treatment for Social Security participants is a matter of particular importance from the standpoint of income distribution, given that Social Security covers just about all workers, including the low-paid, while private pensions provide supplements for only about half of the workforce, and predominantly for the higher-paid at that.

Such a change in investment policy is not necessary to bring the system into long-term balance, which can be accomplished entirely by selecting from the more traditional proposals discussed earlier. But this method of giving workers' contributions to Social Security more financial power offers an attractive alternative to benefit cuts and contribution rate increases, and over the long run greatly improves the ratio of contributions to benefits for long-term contributors. And there is another positive byproduct from having a substantial part of the trust fund buildup invested in equities. To the extent that this is done and funds are not lent to the government in return for government bonds, public confusion is avoided. Today, with the trust fund investing solely in government bonds, this is widely misinterpreted as "Social Security funds are being spent for other purposes" and "Social Security funds are not really contributing to savings."

One way or another, eliminating Social Security's long-range deficit requires generating more income or less outgo. But the methods chosen may affect Social Security participants—including both current beneficiaries and wage-earners and future beneficiaries and wage-earners—very differently. Three of the changes discussed earlier—extending coverage to those state and local employees now excluded (thus increasing income), increasing the taxation of benefits and eliminating the special tax exemption applying only to Social Security beneficiaries, and making the CPI more accurate (thus reducing outgo)—would contribute to restoring long-range balance as a by-product of making the program more equitable. And allowing Social Security to invest directly in equities would result in properly allocating income from the economic contributions made by Social Security and private investments, such as private pensions, and in providing for a fairer distribution of the returns from retirement saving. The remaining proposals discussed above are simply benefit cuts or tax increases. They require sacrifices—but sacrifices that can be broadly shared so that no one group has to sacrifice very much.

Table 2.3 (see pages 24–25) summarizes the major options and their impact on the deficit.

Although I believe it has major disadvantages, another way to eliminate the deficit is to explicitly turn to pay-as-you-go as the long-range plan and institute a schedule of pay-as-you-go tax rate increases in the law. Table 2.4 (see page 26) shows the contribution rates that would be needed based on present benefit and financing provisions (that is, without any of the proposed changes summarized in Table 2.3).

Still another possibility would be a hybrid of partial advance funding and pay-as-you-go, resulting from selecting some of the changes described in Table 2.3 and later, when necessary, introducing a pay-as-you-go contribution rate.

If the changes selected for near-term enactment were those summarized in Table 2.1, reducing the long-range deficit to 0.72 percent of payroll, the contribution rate would need to climb to 7.4 percent of earnings in about 2040 and to 8.1 percent in 2070 (see Table 2.5, page 27). But the contribution-rate increases required under pay-as-you-go financing, even though long postponed under this hybrid approach, share with any tax increase or benefit cut the undesirable effect of worsening the benefit/contribution ratio for younger workers, and the rates are of course higher than needed under partial advance funding.

In March 1998, Senator Daniel Patrick Moynihan of New York, the ranking Democrat on the Senate Finance Committee, proposed modifying Social Security to keep it quite literally and strictly on a pay-as-you-go basis (as he had previously recommended in 1989). He would cut the contribution rate for the employer and for the employee from the current rate of 6.2 percent of earnings to 5.2 percent for the next 30 years,[8] thus preventing any substantial buildup in the fund. Senator Robert Kerrey (D., Neb.) joined in this proposal.

The effect of reducing income to the program over the next 30 years is, of course, to increase the long-range Social Security deficit, bringing it up from the estimated 2.23 percent of payroll under present law to nearly 3 percent. Under a pay-as-you-go approach, this change, by itself, would necessitate very large contribution-rate increases after 2030, rising to over 9 percent by 2070, as shown in Table 2.4.

To avoid such major tax increases over the long run, a strict pay-as-you-go plan would have to make major cuts in benefits. In Senator Moynihan's proposal, the cuts reach 30 percent. To make up for these cuts—at least in part—he proposes to create a voluntary savings plan to be financed by the reduction in Social Security taxes. The worker, whose Social Security tax is reduced by one percentage point under the plan, can choose to put this 1 percent of earnings in a savings plan to be matched by the employer, who also has had a one percentage point reduction in the tax. The employer does not have to pay this 1 percent unless the employee makes the election.

Under a voluntary approach, of course, there is no way of knowing to what extent workers would elect to save rather than spend the 1 percent and thus attract the employer match. Perhaps most of the higher-paid would do so, although many would certainly offset at least part of the 1 percent against saving they are already making. For those who choose to save, the deductions from the worker's earnings plus the employer contribution would, over the next 30 years, equal the 6.2 percent of payroll required under present law for Social Security. But beginning in 2030 the percent of earnings per worker for the two proposals combined would reach 7.2 percent; later, 7.7 percent would be required, with the employer paying a like amount.

Workers who did not elect to save the 1 percent reduction—probably a high percentage of the lower-paid—would suffer the full 30 percent cut in retirement income. For those who did save, the ultimate level of their Social Security-related retirement income would depend on their investment returns. Some might have retirement income greater than promised under the current Social Security system. Others would have less—much less if they had bad luck with their investments. There are no guarantees.

The Moynihan plan would also make several changes that have wide support among Social Security experts and that are essentially the same as those summarized in Table 2.1 and that appear later in my preferred plan (see Table 2.6, page 31, Package 7). With regard to the Cost-of-Living Adjustment, however, the Moynihan plan would go far beyond the anticipated BLS changes to the Consumer Price Index (shown in Table 2.3, Option 3), cutting the CPI rate by a full 1 percent.[9]

TABLE 2.3
OPTIONS TO BRING SOCIAL SECURITY INTO LONG-TERM BALANCE*

Option	Comment	Reduces Deficit**
1. Make the program universal, gradually extending coverage to all full-time state and local government workers hired after 2000.	Most state and local government employees are already covered. The 3.7 million who are not are the last major group in labor force not covered	-0.25
2. Increase the taxation of benefits and drop the special income tax exemption applying only to Social Security beneficiaries.	Benefits should be taxed to the extent they exceed what worker has paid in, as in other contributory defined-benefit plans, and dropping the special exemption would improve income tax equity (lowest-income beneficiaries, about 30% of total, would still be untaxed).	-0.36
3. Change the Social Security Cost of Living Adjustment (COLA) to reflect corrections to the Consumer Price Index (CPI).	With the CPI presently believed to overstate inflation, changes announced by BLS plus annual pricing of the market basket should result in more accurate CPI and smaller COLAs.	-0.42
4. Raise maximum earnings base an additional 2% each year from 2000 to 2009.	At one time, 90% of wages in covered employment were under this base, above which earnings are neither taxed nor credited for benefit-computation purposes. Under present law the base is expected to cover only 84.5% of wages by 2006. This change goes halfway toward the 90% standard, increasing coverage to 87.3%.	-0.27
5. Increase the length of the wage-averaging period for benefit computation purposes from 35 to 38 years.	Current 35-year averaging period is arbitrary and has not been increased since 1991 despite increased longevity of program. Extending it to 38 to 40 years is feasible; extending it to 38 reduces benefits for those becoming eligible in the future by 3% on average.	-0.27
5a. Increase the wage-averaging period from 35 to 40 years.	Reduces future benefits by an average of 5%.	-0.46

Option	Comment	Reduces Deficit**
6. Increase contribution rates by 0.20 percentage points for workers and employers alike and comparably for the self-employed.	It is reasonable to ask workers in the future to contribute modestly to bringing the program into balance. Increase equals deduction of $20 per $10,000 of annual earnings.	-0.37
6a. Increase contribution rates by 0.40 percentage points.	Equals deduction of $40 per $10,000 of annual earnings.	-0.75
7. Modify the benefit formula gradually so as to maintain 1997 real benefit levels at a minimum but cut replacement rates 3% by 2029.	Future beneficiaries should share in sacrifice needed to reach long-term balance by reducing replacement rate, but benefits on into the future should equal or exceed those now being paid to new beneficiaries.	-0.21
7a. Modify formula to cut replacement rates 5%.	As above.	-0.35
8. Increase normal retirement age (NRA) by indexing it to longevity after NRA reaches 67 as scheduled under present law.	If NRA is to be increased at all (see text), this is the most cautious and least harmful approach.	-0.30
9. Apply the Social Security tax on employers to the entire payroll.	There is no good reason to limit the payroll tax on employers to a match with what individual workers are required to pay, since the employer tax can be thought of as going to the support of the entire system.	-1.20
10. Invest part of trust fund in stocks beginning in 2000, reaching 40% of assets in stocks in 2015 and thereafter (assumes ultimate 7% real yield in stocks).	Produces higher return on trust fund investments, giving Social Security participants same advantages as those participating in other pension funds and improving benefit/contribution ratio for younger workers.	-0.92

*There are, of course, other options, such as meeting the entire imbalance with benefit cuts or contribution-rate increases, but the options shown can, in various combinations, accomplish the same purpose with less modification of present-law provisions.

**Assumes an average long-term deficit of 2.23% of payroll as estimated by the Social Security trustees.

TABLE 2.4
PAY-AS-YOU-GO FINANCING: CONTRIBUTION RATES* REQUIRED TO MAINTAIN SOCIAL SECURITY IN LONG-TERM BALANCE WITHOUT OTHER CHANGES

Years	Rate
1996–2024	6.20**
2025–2029	8.00
2030–2049	8.45
2050–2059	8.65
2060–2069	8.90
2070–2079	9.15***

* Rates shown are for deductions from workers' earnings, to be matched by the employer.
** This is the present rate.
*** The rate will continue to rise in following years.

Source: Based on *1997 Annual Report of the Board of Trustees of the Federal Old-Age and Survivors Insurance and Disability Insurance Trust Funds* (Washington, D.C.: Government Printing Office, 1997).

There is much dispute over how much the Consumer Price Index needs to be reduced to make cost-of-living adjustments and automatic adjustments in income tax brackets as accurate as possible. The 1 percent reduction in the Moynihan plan has the support of a study made for the Senate Finance Committee by a group of economists led by Michael Boskin, who chaired the Council of Economic Advisers during the Bush administration. The Bureau of Labor Statistics, which is responsible for the CPI, has improved the measure's accuracy in several ways over the past few years and has announced further changes, but these changes are not nearly as great as that recommended by the Boskin group. Table 2.3, Option 3 reflects the BLS changes and adds a 0.1 percent reduction from more frequent pricing of the CPI market basket.

Social Security's effectiveness in providing a dependable income in retirement is very dependent upon the COLA. Over the course of time, retirees may use up other savings, and the value of private pensions declines because of not being protected against inflation, with the result that low income and impoverishment rise with longevity. Aging widows are particularly at risk of impoverishment. Thus the

TABLE 2.5

MODIFIED PAY-AS-YOU-GO FINANCING: CONTRIBUTION RATES* REQUIRED TO
MAINTAIN SOCIAL SECURITY IN LONG-TERM BALANCE UNDER AN APPROACH
COMBINING PARTIAL ADVANCE FUNDING AND PAY-AS-YOU-GO

Years	Rate
1996–2039	6.20**
2040–2059	7.40
2060–2069	7.80
2070–	8.10***

* Rates shown are for deductions from workers' earnings, to be matched by the
employer.

** This is the present rate (plus any increase selected from Table 2.3).

*** The rate will continue to rise in following years.

Source: Based on *1997 Annual Report of the Board of Trustees of the Federal Old-Age and
Survivors Insurance and Disability Insurance Trust Funds* (Washington, D.C.: Government
Printing Office, 1997).

crucial importance of proceeding with great caution in making any
changes to the CPI, which determines the COLA. The CPI is similar-
ly important in determining income tax brackets. For both of these
reasons, a strong case can be made that any changes to the CPI should
have the support of the experts at BLS or, at the very least, of a strong
consensus of non-BLS experts. That kind of support does not exist for
any changes beyond the 0.42 percent of payroll change shown in
Table 2.3, Option 3. The differences are significant. While a reduction
of the CPI to the extent shown in Table 2.3 has the effect of reducing
Social Security benefits (as compared to present law) about 8 percent by age 85, a reduction to the CPI of 1 percent would reduce
benefits about 21 percent by age 85. And this is not exclusively a
problem for the elderly: Benefits for a worker disabled at age 25
would be reduced 26 percent over 30 years.

The other major way in which the Moynihan plan cuts benefits
is to raise the age of first eligibility for full benefits beyond the age
(67) provided for in present law. (The Moynihan plan is similar in this
respect to Option 8 in Table 2.3, but with a somewhat speeded-up
schedule.)

Those who advocate going to a strict pay-as-you-go plan—by cutting back on the Social Security contribution rate in order to eliminate the buildup of funds that would otherwise take place—usually do so because they fear that the buildup would not be preserved for Social Security but instead would probably be used to support an expansion of other government spending, thus negating the increase in Social Security funds.

Whether government would actually preserve a buildup in Social Security is arguable. Little can be proven one way or another from looking at the past. For example, would general taxes have been higher in recent years if Congress had not had Social Security funds to borrow from? That is an unknown. If Congress did everything it was going to do in any case, then Social Security's buildup kept the national debt from rising even faster and further than it did—in effect saving the Social Security surplus.

Now that Congress has balanced total government income and expenditures, the prospect of exercising the discipline to save any Social Security surplus seems brighter than at any time in the recent past. It would greatly help to clarify the issue, however, if Social Security could not only be declared legally off-budget, as is the case now, but could stand truly apart in the same way that state retirement systems are typically separated from state budgets. This now seems a quite reasonable goal since under present law the non-Social Security budget is predicted by the Office of Management and Budget to come into balance within the next 10 years or so.

In any case, there is broad agreement among Social Security experts that partial advance funding—paying today for some of tomorrow's costs—is highly desirable. With partial advance funding, bringing the program into long-range balance is not very difficult. Senator Moynihan could have easily done so if he had not proposed to increase the long-range imbalance by cutting the contribution rate for the next 30 years. The options in Table 2.1 that have near-consensus support (and that are also included in the Moynihan plan) reduce the estimated long-range deficit from 2.23 percent of payroll to about 0.72 percent of payroll. The remaining imbalance can be brought to zero by making the additional changes shown in Table 2.2 or by various combinations of the proposals shown in Table 2.3. Or, best of all, it can be eliminated simply by combining the consensus items with investing part of the fund buildup in equities (see Table 2.6, page 31, Package 7). Any of these approaches would do the job.

Table 2.6 shows four different packages in addition to the one in Table 2.1 (which would bring the deficit within "close actuarial balance" but not eliminate it) and the one in Table 2.2, Package 2.

There are advantages and disadvantages in each of these groupings (and in the many others that could be developed from Table 2.3). To illustrate: Table 2.2, Package 2 or Table 2.6, Package 3 may be the most attractive of those building on past practices, but Package 4 avoids some of the proposals that would be most likely to draw particular opposition, such as taxing more of the benefit, eliminating the special tax exemption for low-income Social Security beneficiaries, and extending the period over which average wages are computed. On the other hand, it includes further increases in the NRA, which many oppose. Package 5 has no increases in the taxation of benefits or tax increases on employees but will run into major employer objection. Package 6 can avoid taxation of benefits, retain the special income tax exemption for low-income beneficiaries, avoid a benefit cut, and provide for only a small increase in the contribution rate, because it invests part of the accumulating surplus in stocks. Finally, there is the package that I prefer over the others—Package 7.

In addition to eliminating the deficit, all seven packages would increase national savings, just as individual account plans are expected to, and Package 7 by 2015 would be saving about two-thirds as much as the IA plan proposed by Advisory Council chairman Edward Gramlich. If policymakers feel that increasing national savings is a more important goal than holding down deductions from workers' earnings and maintaining benefit levels close to those provided in present law, Social Security can do the job: The buildup in the trust fund can be accelerated by raising contribution rates or reducing benefits more than called for by any of the proposals in Table 2.3. The IA plan achieves greater national savings not by setting up individual accounts but by requiring greater deductions from workers' earnings (in order to fund the new IAs while at the same time continuing to fund Social Security's ongoing albeit reduced obligations). Equivalent deductions from workers' earnings or reductions in benefit amounts within the traditional program would produce the same result in terms of national savings. Personally, I would prefer to seek additional national savings elsewhere, but the point is simply that a decision about higher contribution rates and greater national savings can be arrived at independently of a decision on whether to recommend individual accounts.

TABLE 2.6
RESTORING SOCIAL SECURITY TO LONG-TERM BALANCE:
FIVE ADDITIONAL PACKAGES OF OPTIONS THAT WOULD DO THE JOB
(In addition to those shown in Tables 2.1 and 2.2)

Package 3

Proposal	Number in Table 2.3	Reduces deficit
Adjust COLA to reflect corrections to CPI.	3	-0.42
Extend coverage.	1	-0.25
Increase maximum taxable earnings base.	4	-0.27
Increase contribution rate by 0.40 percentage points.	6a	-0.75
Increase taxation of benefits.	2	-0.36
Change benefit formula to reduce replacement rate by 3%.	7	-0.21

Balance after implementing above changes (*adjusted for interaction of proposals*): -0.03%

Package 4

Proposal	Number in Table 2.3	Reduces deficit
Adjust COLA to reflect corrections to CPI.	3	-0.42
Extend coverage.	1	-0.25
Increase maximum taxable earnings base.	4	-0.27
Increase contribution rate by 0.40 percentage points.	6a	-0.75
Change benefit formula to reduce replacement rate by 5%.	7a	-0.35
Index NRA to life expectancy after age-67 NRA is reached under present law (not recommended, but has broad support).	8	-0.30

Balance after implementing above changes (*adjusted for interaction of proposals*): +0.50%

Package 5

Proposal	Number in Table 2.3	Reduces deficit
Adjust COLA to reflect corrections to CPI.	3	-0.42
Extend coverage.	1	-0.25
Change benefit formula to reduce replacement rate by 5%.	7a	-0.35
Apply tax on employers to entire payroll.	9	-1.20

Balance after implementing above changes (*adjusted for interaction of proposals*): -0.11%

Package 6

Proposal	Number in Table 2.3	Reduces deficit
Adjust COLA to reflect corrections to CPI.	3	-0.42
Extend coverage.	1	-0.25
Increase maximum taxable earnings base.	4	-0.27
Increase contribution rate by 0.20 percentage points.	6	-0.37
Invest part of the trust fund in stocks.	10	-0.92

Balance after implementing above changes (*adjusted for interaction of proposals*): -0.03%

TABLE 2.6 CONT.		
Package 7 **(Recommended Proposal)**	**Number in** **Table 2.3**	**Reduces** **deficit**
Adjust COLA to reflect corrections to CPI.	3	-0.42
Extend coverage.	1	-0.25
Increase taxation of benefits.	2	-0.36
Increase wage-averaging period from 35 to 38 years.	5	-0.27
Increase maximum earnings base.	4	-0.27
Invest part of the trust fund in stocks.	10	-0.92

Balance after implementing above changes (*adjusted for interaction of proposals*): +0.10%

Among the important conclusions to be drawn from this discussion are these: (1) substituting partial advance funding for pay-as-you-go keeps down the ultimate contribution rate, improves the benefit/contribution ratio for younger workers, and improves national savings; (2) there are several ways to bring the program into long-range balance while maintaining it as a fully defined-benefit program continuing to follow the same basic principles as in the past; (3) the system can be brought into balance for the next 50 years and trust fund exhaustion postponed from 2030 to 2050 largely by program changes that are desirable in any case from the standpoint of improving equity; (4) a future benefit cut of 5 percent (in addition to taxing benefits as other defined-benefit contributory plans are taxed) is the most that needs to be considered under any acceptable plan and much less of a cut is all that is required under several plans; (5) a contribution rate increase of 0.4 percentage points on both employers and employees is the most that needs to be considered, and much less is all that is required under several acceptable plans; and, finally, (6) investing part of Social Security's trust fund accumulations could avoid tax increases on earnings and all but a small cut in benefits.

In summary, it can be stated categorically that there are many acceptable ways of bringing the present Social Security system into long-range balance without departing from the major principles that have been responsible for the program's great success. It is not at all necessary to turn to compulsory saving and private accounts because of the deficit in the existing system. In fact, as discussed in Chapter 4, there are major problems in cutting back on the basic government program and substituting compulsory saving for part of the basic protection now furnished by the traditional Social Security system.

3

SOCIAL SECURITY'S 75-YEAR COST ESTIMATES

There are several issues related to relying on 75-year estimates as the measure of long-term balance that need discussion. These include an evaluation of what can be expected of 75-year estimates and why such a long period is chosen in the first place; why, in spite of the length of the period we need, nevertheless, to think beyond any particular set of 75-year estimates; and why we need a fail-safe provision in the law to deal with the possibility that changed assumptions in the future may move the long-range balance either way—up or down.

Not all of the uneasiness about Social Security financing is due to the misunderstandings discussed in Chapter 1 of this report. One reason for the erosion of public confidence is that several times over the past 30 years the long-range estimates have changed substantially and, in each case, after modifications have been made in the system to meet the revised estimates of cost, the public has been assured that now the system is soundly financed for the long run—only to discover within a few years that the estimates have been changed again and a new deficit is being predicted.

After the 1972 amendments were enacted, the program was said to be soundly financed for 75 years, but in a short time the Trustees reported it to be out of balance because of the unexpectedly high inflation caused by the first oil crisis and changes in long-range economic assumptions. Important changes in financing were enacted in 1977, after which the program was said to be in financial balance for the next 50 years. But the even higher rates of inflation triggered by the second oil crisis in 1979 undermined the financing plan, and a highly publicized rescue mission was conducted by the National Commission on Social Security Reform (the Greenspan Commission), culminating in the 1983 amendments. At that time President Reagan, members of the commission, and both liberal and conservative congressmen and senators once more pronounced the system in balance for the traditional 75-year period. But within little more than a decade the Trustees were reporting, once again, that the program faced a long-term deficit. It is not surprising that as people now look at various proposals to bring the system into balance, some ask, "Why should we believe you've got it right this time?"

Maintaining long-range balance has not always been a problem. Prior to the 1972 amendments, which introduced automatic cost-of-living increases and several other automatic provisions, the long-range cost estimates had a major built-in safety factor. Specific assumptions were made, as they are today, about future fertility rates, mortality rates, marriage rates and many other demographic factors that affect cost, but no attempt was made to predict the future movement of wages and prices.

For the purpose of estimating, it was assumed that wages and prices would remain unchanged indefinitely—in other words, that there would be no real growth in wages. No one really expected this to be the case, of course, but the assumption was a good hedge. When, in fact, wages did increase faster than prices, as they generally have, the old cost estimates proved to be too conservative, and a surplus was reported. This surplus was first used to absorb any changes in cost resulting from any less favorable assumptions that might have been substituted for earlier assumptions, and then any remaining surplus was used to update benefit levels to help keep them abreast of the increases in wages and prices.

This process was repeated over and over without triggering any widespread public concern about long-range costs. However, after the law was changed so that benefits and many other program features moved automatically in relation to increasing prices and wages, there was no longer a rationale for basing estimates on an assumption that wages and prices would remain level. Indeed, the estimates needed to incorporate assumptions about their future movements. Thus the safety factor was lost. We need something to take its place.

Of course, future trends may have the effect of making the system less expensive than currently estimated. Over the past two decades, the assumptions upon which the estimates are based have become increasingly conservative as a reflection of the dramatic decline in real wage growth (going from an assumption of real wage growth of 2.5 percent annually to 1.5 percent and now to 0.9 percent). If this trend is even slightly reversed over the next 75 years, program revenues would be higher than currently estimated. And there are many other factors that could move either way—fertility rates, mortality rates, and immigration rates being among the most important. The one certainty is that a 75-year estimate can never get it exactly right. Think how things would have turned out if, in 1923, during the administration of President Harding, experts had tried to forecast population growth and the movement of wages and prices up to 1998. Among other things, they could not have anticipated the impact of a worldwide depression, a second global war, and an unprecedented cold war.

The fact is that there is no way to make anything like an accurate prediction of costs and income over a 75-year span, and indeed the Trustees don't really attempt such a forecast. They make, first, high-cost and low-cost estimates, which differ greatly over the 75-year period and either of which could turn out to be close to reality or far off, and then they turn to a middle-range estimate—a best-guess estimate—and use it for all practical purposes as if it were the only estimate. In reality they have no other choice. In a self-financed, contributory program, a particular set of estimates has to be selected as a basis for establishing contribution rates. The best-guess estimates are selected for this purpose and then become the basis for just about all discussions of costs.

Unfortunately, a misleading sense of precision is conveyed by the process because the estimates are, of necessity, carried out to two decimal points. For example, the Trustees' current best-guess estimate is that Social Security will be out of balance by an average of 2.23 percent of payroll over the 75-year period, and proposals to bring it into balance (including the ones discussed here) add up, one by one, to precisely reach this seemingly exact figure. But again there isn't any real choice. To assign a long-run saving or cost to a change of any magnitude quickly requires getting into two decimal points. Sophisticated observers realize that these long-range cost estimates can be only the roughest kind of a comparison of income and outgo over such a long period of time, but the media and the public are left with an unrealistic impression of exactitude, which then makes the public-confidence problem that much worse when these seemingly precise calculations turn out to be only best-guesses that require periodic revision.

So why make 75-year estimates if they cannot be relied on as accurate predictors? First, they are an expression of the intent to continue Social Security as a self-supporting system. There is no other way for Congress to make this point so convincingly as to plan ahead and include in the law contribution rates designed to make the program self-supporting over a period that roughly encompasses the entire working life and retirement of young people just entering the labor market.

Second, many current provisions and virtually all proposals for change require decades before they are fully phased in, so long-range estimates are needed to get any kind of feel for the full cost of proposed changes. To make changes based on assumptions about what will happen only during the next decade or two could be grossly misleading.

Third, this approach has the advantage of anticipating problems before they arrive and alerting policymakers to the need for action when it is easiest to make adjustments. Even though long-range estimates cannot ever be "right" except by the wildest of coincidences, they can warn us of potential, albeit distant, pitfalls. So, great care is taken to make the estimates as reasonable as possible and to report on them fully to Congress and the public.

The Trustees report annually and in great detail, and their conclusions, particularly if they point to problems ahead, receive major press attention. Other groups, including official advisory councils and various unofficial organizations, also frequently report on Social Security long-range financing, generating additional media coverage. The pattern has been that, as assumptions about long-range trends and the Trustees' estimates change, the system is widely reported to be in or out of balance or to have increasing or decreasing deficits; Congress takes notice; and adjustments are made, sometimes decades before they are actually needed. There are no last-minute surprises in Social Security financing, and this is as it should be in a program that has been correctly called "the largest trusteeship in the history of the world." (With the exception of Canada, no other national system of social insurance uses such long-range estimates—and several nations have had to struggle with serious financial imbalances that overtook their systems without much warning.)

We need to continue to make 75-year estimates just as in the past, but they should be presented with more emphasis on the process of constantly reassessing the assumptions and bringing them up to date with the latest information as it develops, so that the media and the public understand that Social Security costs, just like those of any public or private program with long-range consequences, are subject to continual reevaluation—a process that should not, in and of itself, cause undue anxiety, especially once a fail-safe provision is included in the law to accommodate any long-term imbalance that might develop.

We must also recognize that a complete solution for the long-term financing of Social Security requires that the program be balanced not only over the 75-year period immediately ahead but that it remain in balance for *successive* 75-year periods—that is, 75-year estimates made next year, or five years hence, or 25 years from now. Rightly or not, it is currently assumed that life expectancies continue to rise indefinitely. That being the case, in the out years of each new 75-year period over which estimates are successively made the estimates will show more and more longer-living, elderly beneficiaries receiving benefits, while the number of wage-earners paying in will not keep pace. This assumption alone, unless offset by changes in other assumptions, produces a slight but regular increase in estimated costs for each successive 75-year estimating period. Consequently, with present funding arrangements the program may be in balance for the 75 years following 1998, say, but not for the 75 years from 2010 to 2085 or from 2025 to 2100. Unless the program is financed so that the trust fund is increasing rather than declining at the end of a 75-year period, the Trustees will soon be reporting once again that Social Security over the long run has insufficient funds to continue to pay full benefits on time.

The several packages of options previously discussed can restore Social Security to long-term balance—that is, within the current 75-year estimating period. To make sure that the trust fund is building up at the end of 75 years, however, it will be necessary in conjunction with these proposals to schedule a tax increase toward the end of the period. Otherwise the packages described would show a declining trust fund at the end of the 75-year period. I would suggest, therefore,

that consideration be given to scheduling, in addition to any contribution-rate increase chosen from among the alternatives discussed
above, an increase effective in 2050 of 0.80 percent of earnings for
employees matched by employers.

The 7 percent rate to be charged indefinitely beginning in 2050 is
well below the pay-as-you-go rate of 8.65 percent that would be needed in 2050 (see Chapter 2, Table 2.4) and would still be below it even
if another 0.4 percent deducted from workers' earnings and matched by
employers were added (the largest contribution-rate increase in any of
the alternatives discussed in Chapter 2).[1] Of course, the 2050 rate
increase would not be allowed to go into effect unless cost estimates
made as the effective date approaches show a need for it.

Finally, we need a safety factor—a hedge like the old level-wage
assumption—to accommodate any future changes in the estimates.
The 2050 rate increase described above can serve this purpose. If, as
2050 approaches, the program appears likely to cost less than is now
being estimated, the scheduled increase could be moved further into
the future. Conversely, if the system is estimated to be more expensive
than previously thought, the 2050 increase could be moved up to an
earlier year.

With the 2050 rate increase serving the dual function of providing a fail-safe and making sure that the trust fund is increasing at the
end of the 75-year period, the system would under almost all fore-
seeable circumstances stay in balance over the whole 75 years, requiring only an adjustment in the effective date of the tax-rate increase
already provided for.[2] We would avoid the erosion of public confidence that now follows virtually any statement by the Trustees to the
effect that the system requires substantial shoring up, because this
possibility would already have been taken into account and written
into the law in the form of a rate increase scheduled far in advance.
Of course, in the unlikely event that the estimated long-range costs
increased so much that they could not be met in this way, Congress
would have to decide whether to enact further tax increases and/or
benefit cuts.

One other aspect of Social Security's long-range financing
requires attention. Although in practice Social Security has been
largely pay-as-you-go, collecting only enough to pay current benefits and maintain a contingency reserve, the law in the past has
contained scheduled future rate increases that would have resulted
in partial advance funding had they been allowed to go into effect.

Thus the system, while charging only a current pay-as-you-go rate, has been able to project a long-range balance because of a contribution schedule that later on would have produced a large fund with substantial earnings.

No clear-cut policy decision has ever been made regarding whether to stay indefinitely with pay-as-you-go in practice or move to partial advance funding by building an earnings reserve larger than a contingency fund—that is, a reserve large enough to make a significant contribution to long-range financing. A decision to stay with pay-as-you-go while still requiring full self-financing for the program would have meant a big increase in the ultimate rate in the law. In effect, we have been following a pay-as-you-go policy without facing up to the long-range consequences of continuing with such a policy. This ad hoc approach has been expedient, perhaps, but it has also been misleading. I believe that we should explicitly adopt a set policy of partial advance funding, and the proposals put forward in Chapter 2 as alternative solutions for the long term are based on this policy.

4

PARTIAL PRIVATIZATION OF SOCIAL SECURITY: THE DRAWBACKS OF INDIVIDUAL ACCOUNTS

Many proposals to privatize Social Security are currently under discussion. Some, such as the plan proposed by the Cato Institute, would substitute a privatized system for the entire Social Security system. Another approach, exemplified by the Personal Security Accounts (PSA) plan supported by five members of the 1994–96 Advisory Council, would reduce the government-operated program eventually to the payment of low flat benefits, substituting a compulsory savings program with individual accounts for the rest of what we know as Social Security today. These are radical proposals, and I believe that they have little chance of enactment.

It is more likely that serious consideration will be given to proposals that would shrink the present Social Security system to make room for an individual account plan—leaving the core system *looking* much like the present program, only smaller. When contrasted with major privatization schemes, plans such as the Individual Accounts (IA) plan of Advisory Council chairman Edward Gramlich, or the plan proposed by Senator Moynihan, may be seen by some as acceptable compromises.[1] They really are not. In order to bring the residual Social Security program into long-range balance while at the same time funding the new system of individual accounts, they have to reduce benefits under the residual program by 30 percent on average. In other words, they replace nearly a third of Social Security's defined-benefit protection with a defined-contribution scheme—compulsory in the case of Gramlich, voluntary in the case of Moynihan—and thus weaken the foundation of our national retirement income system.

The IA plan creates a new system of individual savings accounts. Workers and employers would continue to contribute to the present system at the current level of deductions from workers' earnings (6.2 percent), with their contributions matched by employers. However, since the income produced at this combined contribution rate of 12.4 percent of payroll would not be sufficient to maintain the present program in balance over the long run, Social Security benefits would be gradually scaled back—ultimately by 30 percent for the average worker, 22 percent for the lower-paid, and 32 percent for the higher-paid.[2] In addition to contributing 6.2 percent of their earnings to the present system, workers would have an additional 1.6 percent of their earnings deducted (with no employer match) to fund their individual accounts. The goal would be for the earnings from investing these accounts to offset, at least on average, the reduction in Social Security benefits.

Under this approach, in other words, workers would be required to set aside more of their earnings than at present to fund a two-part system in which the ultimate level of combined benefits is determined not by law but by the investment earnings from the funds they select.[3] Behind the IA plan is a political calculation—that workers would be very reluctant to accept a tax increase to strengthen the present Social Security system but *would* accept an increase in deductions from their wages as long as it is earmarked for an individual account that they are expected to regard as their own, notwithstanding strict rules preventing access to the account before reaching retirement age.

The IA plan also assumes that workers would prefer to rely to some extent on their own investment skills (choosing from a menu of government-overseen investment options) rather than on a defined-benefit retirement program in which it is the government's responsibility to see that benefits defined by law are paid. Risk is present in either situation, but in Social Security the risk is broadly shared, while in individual accounts the risk is borne by the individual. Behind the

IA plan, in short, is an untested assumption that wage-earners setting aside funds for retirement would prefer to bear part of the risk individually rather than share risk in a system for which all of the participants are collectively responsible.

Proponents argue that the IA approach will, *on average,* protect present benefit levels for Social Security participants by bringing the combined benefits of the reduced Social Security system and the new savings plan up to the level now provided for, but not fully funded by, the present Social Security system. But many participants would, of course, receive less than average returns on their investments, so their combined benefits would be less than under present law.[4] And the young disabled, in particular, would lose: With their wages typically cut off or at least curtailed by disability, they could not expect to benefit very much from the compulsory savings plan, but as the program developed, Social Security benefits for the disabled would be reduced by 30 percent on average.

The inescapable fact is that the IA plan would reduce Social Security's defined benefit in the long run by 30 percent for the average worker, replacing the diminished benefit with the *hope* that the *average* return on savings in individual accounts would make up for the loss. But even if this turned out to be the case *on average,* many participants, particularly the lower-paid, would fall below the average. As Herbert Stein, who chaired the President's Council of Economic Advisers in President Nixon's administration, wrote last year in the *Wall Street Journal* (February 5, 1997): "It is not sufficient to say that some people who are very smart or very lucky in the management of their funds will have high incomes and those who are not will have low incomes and that everything will average out."

There are other problems with the IA approach:

- ◆ **The plan puts workers at increased risk.** A major objection to replacing part of Social Security with individual accounts is that it increases risk for the individual—which, while appropriate for supplementary protection, is questionable policy for Social Security, the basic floor of retirement protection. In addition to the general risk of picking funds that perform poorly, workers would also be exposed to a timing risk—the risk of beginning or ending an investment period in a bad market. They would have to start investing when they first become employed and then convert to a benefit when they retire. As noted previously, they would be able to choose equities or bonds and make transfers between the two, but they would not know ahead of time when to invest in equities and when to get out of the market (although, of course, they might choose to increase their bond holdings as they neared retirement). Market fluctuations would be beyond their control, and Figure 4.1 by Gary Burtless of The Brookings Institution shows the enormous variation in replacement rates (the percentage of past earnings that a pension represents) that could result solely because of the timing of retirement within very brief periods of time—going, for example, from 47 percent in 1980 to 68 percent in 1981, then back down to 42 percent in 1993, then back up to 72 percent in 1997.[5]

FIGURE 4.1
EARNINGS REPLACEMENT RATES OF WORKERS WITH 40-YEAR CAREERS WHO INVEST IN U.S. STOCK MARKET AND RETIRE, 1912–1997

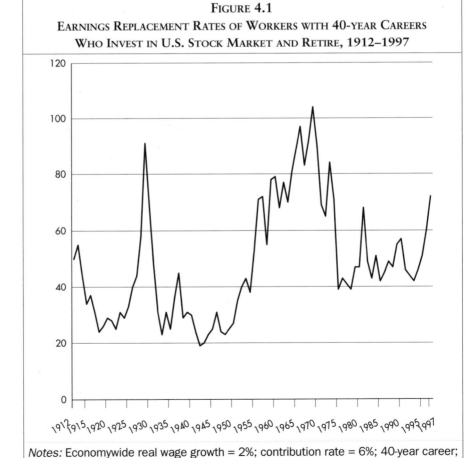

Notes: Economywide real wage growth = 2%; contribution rate = 6%; 40-year career; invest in stocks over 40-year career; convert to level annuity at age 62.

Source: Unpublished figure prepared by Gary Burtless, The Brookings Institution.

Variations of this magnitude would represent a serious problem for workers, whose expectations of retirement income could be abruptly undercut. A 58-year-old worker in 1970, looking at the 90-percent replacement rate going to a 65-year-old retiree in that year, would be shocked to discover seven years later that his own pension would be pegged at a replacement rate of 41 percent—less than half as much as expected. There would be little he could do about it other than settle for much less retirement income than anticipated or keep working in hopes that replacement rates would rise. His situation would be even worse if, in 1969, Congress had looked at the 104-percent replacement rate made possible by the then-bull market and opted to cut back on contributions to these accounts. By 1977, with replacement rates plummeting, elected officials would be inundated with complaints about hardship among the elderly and pleas to fill in the gap. Looking at this illustration of what might have been, it seems clear that dissatisfaction with the vagaries of a system of individual accounts could have wide-ranging and long-lasting repercussions.

- **The plan promises more than it can deliver.** Even on average, the plan would be unlikely to achieve the goal of adequate retirement income because it seems inevitable that over time the savings account holders would be allowed access to their accounts for purposes unrelated to retirement, with the result that many would spend much of the money in the account prior to retirement. After all, a major selling point for IAs is that the money "belongs" to the individual. IA-holders facing health emergencies, tuition payments, or other major expenses would want access to their "own" funds in such situations. Based on experience with IRAs and 401(k) plans, it can be confidently predicted that political leaders would acquiesce. Once early access is permitted, many IAs would be substantially reduced by the time the account-holder reaches retirement.

- **Public support for Social Security might be undermined.** The residual Social Security system would produce lower and lower benefits as time went on, while individual reports on investment returns would show growing accumulations, even in those cases where the returns would actually be quite low, reinforcing the impression that IAs were "better." Many workers might press to change the law in order to allow more of their contributions to be shifted from Social Security into private accounts. If that were to happen, the redistributional capabilities of the present system would be lost. The weighted Social Security benefit formula favoring the low-paid, which has been so successful in reducing poverty and near-poverty among the elderly, is not likely to be maintained in a system made up largely of individual accounts. On the other hand, a parallel government system of flat benefits high enough to make a major impact on poverty is likely to be means-tested, regardless of the specifications proposed by sponsors.

- **The plan would reduce the living standard of low wage earners.** The IA plan would increase national savings—as indeed do all three of the plans proposed in the Advisory Council report—but most of the increase would come from the lower-paid. Present savers—mostly above-average earners—would tend to decrease the saving that they had been doing voluntarily to offset the new requirements. It is difficult to judge how much net additional saving would come from them. Most of the increase would probably come from low-wage workers who are not saving now; this is where the new compulsion hits and there is no relief. Is it really desirable to force more saving from the lower-paid for the purpose of increasing their cash income in retirement even beyond the level of promised Social Security benefits? Probably not. Many lower-paid workers live from payday to payday and have a more immediate need for health insurance—or to pay for more basic needs such as adequate shelter, food, and clothing—than to set aside more of their earnings exclusively for retirement.

- **The IA approach makes solving Medicare's financial problems harder by preempting increases in compulsory deductions from workers' earnings for retirement savings rather than for health care.** Putting this another way, if a significant additional deduction from earnings of the kind required by the IA plan were to be seriously considered, there would be a more immediate need to direct at least part of the income to Medicare or to health insurance generally rather than to retirement income alone.

- **The plan weakens our three-tier retirement system.** Social Security, as the foundation of that system—augmented by supplementary private pensions and individual savings—is, appropriately, a defined-benefit plan with benefits determined by law rather than by the risks and unpredictability of individual investments. Partial privatization would shift Social Security toward becoming a defined-*contribution* plan, in which benefits are dependent upon how contributions are invested. This is a particularly bad idea now, since private pension plans are increasingly of the defined-contribution type, such as 401(k) plans. Taking risks with supplementary protection is reasonable only if the base is secure. If Social Security is not itself maintained as a defined-benefit plan, a worker's entire retirement package is subject to the risk of market returns.

◆   **The plan weakens disability protection even more than retirement protection.** Changing the benefit formula from 90 percent, 32 percent, and 15 percent of average indexed earnings to 90 percent, 22.4 percent, and 10.5 percent under the IA plan would have a disproportionate impact on the disabled, because as a general rule the disabled have lower incomes than retirees. They are less likely to have private pensions or insurance benefits to augment Social Security and are less likely to be able to get and keep part-time work, so they must rely on Social Security to provide a relatively large share of their total income.

Further, disabled workers typically have much smaller asset holdings than retirees. This reflects two of the realities experienced by disabled workers: Their careers are cut short before they have accumulated savings to supplement Social Security, and they face new disability-related expenses. Unlike retirees, whose regular living expenses may decline when their working-years-related expenses decline, living costs for persons with disabilities may rise after they leave the labor force. Over time disability benefits, like retirement benefits, are cut 30 percent for the average worker but the compulsory saving plan is much less likely to make up for the loss. For workers who are disabled while young the compulsory saving plan is just about useless.

◆   **The plan could lead to new labor relations problems.** Cutting Social Security's defined benefits would likely cause friction between employers and employees. Virtually all private and public pension plans are built on the assumption that the retiree will also receive Social Security. And pension arrangements, at least at large firms, have usually been worked out over the years with employee representatives; pensions are part of the overall compensation bargaining process. What would happen to these plans if the basic Social Security benefit were to be gradually cut by an average of 30 percent? At the very least, we could expect a long period of uncertainty and unrest. Would private plans have to make up the difference—particularly for older workers—as Social Security is scaled back? Unions would certainly want to protect workers by retaining the equivalent of present Social Security promises in defined pension benefits, and employers would just as certainly resist. The stakes would be high. Moreover, all the pension integration rules would have to be changed, since the effect of the weighted benefit formula would be reduced, and these changes could result in significant increases in private pension costs.

No doubt many workers would find it appealing, at least initially, to have their own accounts—particularly because of the widespread misconception that major cuts in benefits and major increases in taxes are necessary to put the present system back into balance. But many presumably would not want to bother with individual accounts if they were more confident of the long-term stability of the present Social Security system. Some of those initially attracted to IAs would feel less enthusiastic as they learned of the trade-offs—in essence, a stronger sense of personal "ownership" (albeit with limited assets and limited control of investment choices and annuity options) versus the risk of ending up with less security—and particularly as they learn more about their personal stake in the present system.

Thanks to an amendment sponsored by Senator Moynihan some years ago, workers are already becoming better informed about what they can expect from Social Security. The Social Security Administration has distributed Personal Earnings and Benefit Statements (PEBES) to millions of workers (starting with those nearing retirement age and working down from there), and beginning in 1999 will send annual statements to all workers over 25 for whom mailing addresses are available—expected to be about 122 million people out of the expected 140 million workers in covered employment. This represents a huge step forward in the dissemination of important information to Social Security participants. Suddenly, the benefits of the present system are becoming more tangible.

ADMINISTERING THE IA PLAN:
A MAJOR CHALLENGE FOR EMPLOYERS AND GOVERNMENT

In assessing the pros and cons of partial privatization, it is also important to focus on what has been perhaps the least closely examined aspect of the IA approach: the difficulties that employers and the government would face in administering such a plan.

The administrative challenges are substantial. At a minimum, employers would need to deduct the additional 1.6 percent from earnings each payday and forward the amounts to the government identified in such a way that they could be correctly deposited to an individual's account in one or more of the government-sponsored funds. Information about the choices available would need to be furnished to employees and their fund choices communicated to the government. Individual records would need to be kept of all deposits and their earnings and reported to employees, who would also need to be given opportunities to periodically change their allocation of investments. And it would be necessary to correct reporting errors and to reconcile differences between employers' reports and employee claims of errors. The government at a minimum would need to see that all this happens—and, in addition, to ensure that funds deposited in individual accounts are retained to retirement and then converted to government-sponsored indexed annuities.

Some of the operational problems that would accompany the implementation of any individual-account plan are suggested by the following commentary by Josh S. Weston, chairman of Automatic Data Processing, on a partial-privatization proposal developed by a Committee for Economic Development (CED) panel (Mr. Weston, who also chairs CED's Research and Policy Committee, was a member of the panel and generally supports the proposal):

> This [CED] report does not address the many complex administrative issues involved in processing funds for 140 million individual retirement accounts, each of which permits employees to designate contributions to more than one fund. The task would be massive not only because of the size of the labor force but also because of the frequent changes in employment status. Over one third of all workers—about 40 to 50 million individuals—change their employer or employment status (e.g., employed to not employed) each year.

Adding to the administrative complexity would be the need for a reliable, timely system for crediting accrued interest and dividends to each employee's several funds each month and executing transfers between funds.

The report also does not address how fund administrators would be chosen and their number. There is no likely way, in my view, that an environment of multiple administrators, chosen by either the fund managers, employers, or employees, could handle this very complex movement of monies, investments, and employers. The only credible solution would be a single private, regulated administrator for all PRA [Personal Retirement Accounts] accounts and funds. The Federal Thrift Savings Plan is in many ways a good model, although it is a public entity and permits transfers among funds only once per month. The two current public administration systems that affect all employees are the Social Security Administration and the Internal Revenue Service. Neither is sufficiently timely, nimble, and accurate to serve as a national PRA administrator.[6]

One might add that no private administrator has ever had experience with a task of this magnitude. The numbers involved are very large: 6 million employers and more than 140 million individual accounts—approximately 133 million for employees and 8 million for the self—employed.[7] Nothing comparable to the IA plan has ever been undertaken by any retirement income plan. In comparison, when the federal Thrift Savings Plan (TSP) was started, about 3 million federal employees needed to be informed of their eligibility to participate and advised about their TSP investment options. And TIAA-CREF, a large manager of private defined-contribution plans with participant-directed accounts, encompasses about 6,000 employers and 1.5 million participating employees. These are very small undertakings in comparison to the scope of the IA proposal.

How the necessary tasks described above are parceled out among employers and government is of enormous importance to the parties involved and could well determine both the political viability of the plan and its success or failure in actual operation. What should employers be required to do? Their participation in helping inform their employees could be of great help to government, but would they resist such a requirement? And, of particular importance, would they be willing to make more frequent reports than are now required?

Employers now pay Social Security taxes and transmit withheld income tax continually throughout the year, but only the annual W–2 statement individualizes these taxes. In the case of voluntary 401(k) payroll-deduction savings plans, employers are required to deposit funds withheld in any given month no later than the 15th business day of the next month. Contributions by federal employees partici-pating in the TSP must be deposited every two weeks or on payday. Are employers now going to be required to follow similar rules and identify by payday or on a monthly basis how much has been withheld from a particular worker so that the funds can be promptly allocated and invested in order to start earning returns as soon as possible? More frequent reporting would be a major increase in responsibility for many employers over what they now do for Social Security.

In the past, employers were required to provide information for Social Security purposes on individual employees on a quarterly basis, but widespread employer dissatisfaction with this requirement even-tually prompted Congress to change many Social Security provisions in order to accommodate a system of annual reporting. Employers already administering 401(k) plans might not have major objections to more frequent reporting, but the much larger number of employ-ers who do not offer such plans—particularly small employers—could find such new reporting requirements burdensome and expensive. Would employers also be expected to explain investment choices to employees and be involved in their decisions? What happens if the information provided by employers is inaccurate? What happens if the employer is late or makes mistakes in reporting and the employee loses investment earnings as a result? Will employers be held respon-sible? And how will the costs of administration by government be covered?

Most employers are small. Although employers are encouraged to report W–2s to Social Security electronically (and are required to do so if they employ 250 or more employees), about 5 million of the slightly more than 6 million employers paying Social Security taxes still compile and file their W–2 reports on paper. Many, if not most, of the employers in this category might be expected to object to adding sub-stantially to what they have to do now under the annual reporting system.

It thus seems likely that to avoid employer opposition the IA plan would be modified to permit annual reporting to continue. This could be done, but not without loss for employees. One approach would be to have all the deductions from workers' earnings invested for a year in a single default fund (probably a fund investing only in low-yield but safe long-term government bonds) without employee designation. The employee's designated investment choice could then be followed for future deductions and the original investment redirected as the employee wished. (It can also be assumed that some employees would not make designations promptly, if ever, in which case deductions from their wages could go to the same safe but low-return fund.) But whenever the employee wanted to make a change in the allocation among funds there would be the same lag before the change could be carried out. This annualized approach might make the plan more acceptable to employers, but employees would lose some control over their investments, would earn less investment income on average, and would be faced with the loss of earnings for a period on changing investment designations.[8]

Another possibility might be to do what the British do with their voluntary system: Have the government collect the withholding each payday but invest in a designated fund only once a year. The government benefits from the float, and rationalizes it as a way of meeting its administrative expenses.

These adjustments can be made, but there is no way to avoid putting responsibility on employers for accurately reporting employee deductions, participating in the process of correcting errors, and responding to what employees believe to be errors. And the standard for accuracy will be higher than in the case of the present Social Security system because every dollar deducted from an employee's wages will "belong" to that individual—whereas in Social Security, where the benefit is based on averaging the highest 35 years of earnings, a single error in wage reporting may have little, if any, effect.

Long experience with reporting to Social Security suggests that the burden of correcting errors will be disproportionately borne by smaller employers and that error rates will be significant. In Social Security, error rates are higher for W–2s compiled on paper than for W–2s prepared electronically. The annual combined error rate—that is, the percentage of wage items that cannot be credited to an account—is initially about 3 percent. What this means is that each year some 6 million W–2s cannot be promptly processed and credited to individual earnings records because of errors in reporting names and Social Security numbers. The Social Security Administration, after contacting employers and/or employees, is able to reduce the error rate to about 2 percent. This still represents nearly 5 million unresolved cases, which largely carry over and accumulate from year to year. And these error rates do not include errors resulting from failure to file or from misreporting the amounts withheld. Many of these additional mistakes are likely to develop into investigations as employees find wage items missing from the Social Security reports they are now receiving as a result of the Moynihan amendment, or as taxpayers seek W–2s to support their income tax returns.

Although correcting errors would, of course, be important to beneficiaries, in many cases the exercise would not be cost-effective because the amounts at stake would be so small. Error rates are likely to be highest among the lowest-paid workers, simply because they typically work for smaller employers who are more likely than major employers to misreport withholding. For workers with annual taxable earnings at or below, say, $8,400 a year—about 42 million workers, a third of all workers currently covered by Social Security—the 1.6 percent IA set-aside would, at most, amount to $134 annually, or $11.15 per month. An error rate of 3 percent would mean that at any given moment the IA accounts of more than 1.2 million workers within the lowest-paid category would be subject to adjustment, but because their IA set-asides are so small, the average administrative cost of correcting an IA withholding error for them could easily be greater than the amount in dispute.

This raises a related issue. In weighing the administrative burdens of partial privatization, a major unaddressed question is whether the benefits paid by the savings plan will seem worthwhile to a large number of the employees involved. The amounts going into individual accounts in most cases would be quite small. Among workers covered by Social Security, 56 percent have annual taxable earnings of $18,000 or less, for which the annual IA contribution, at 1.6 percent, would be $288 or less. Average annual earnings among all workers covered are about $26,000, producing a deduction of $416 at 1.6 percent.

At the same time, many higher-paid workers familiar with 401(k) plans might compare the returns, restrictions, and limitations of their IAs unfavorably with their 401(k)s. Contributions to 401(k) plans are voluntary; employees can drop out or defer payments; employers often make matching contributions; many 401(k) plans can be borrowed against; and 401(k) funds can be withdrawn when an employee changes jobs or decides to use the funds for purposes other than retirement, such as medical emergencies or tuition payments (subject to a 10 percent tax penalty). (Although few if any of these features are envisioned for IA accounts, it seems likely that employees would agitate for them—particularly for the right to have access to their IA funds in emergencies—and that, as suggested earlier, policymakers would sooner or later accommodate these demands. In that case, of course, administration of the funds would become more complex, and the income stream in retirement would be reduced as more workers withdrew funds for other purposes.)

There are additional IA administrative costs that should be examined. Looking narrowly at start-up costs, it can be assumed that a major effort would have to be made to familiarize workers with their investment options, an effort that would need to be ongoing in order to respond to employees' questions and to reach employees newly entering the labor market. How much would employers be asked to do? If employers were not expected to help employees understand the plan and their choices, and this job were assigned entirely to Social Security, for example, the cost for district offices could be large and hard to predict. The first wave of inquiries presumably could be dealt with by setting up and staffing an 800 number, but many people would want to talk things over in person—and that goes double, at least at first, for questions about the IA status reports that would be periodically sent to each employee. Many would come to Social Security seeking clarification.

Of course, major employers might elect to help their employees whether required to do so or not. It is common now for personnel departments of major employers to take responsibility for helping employees with the requirements of Social Security claims filing and income tax withholding, and there would be a price to pay in good will if employers just turned off inquiries about a government-required savings plan. But giving advice also carries a cost when the employee thinks the advice has been bad.

Most small employers would want to avoid taking on any additional administrative responsibilities, but regardless of whether they were expected to help employees navigate the IA plan, they would have to report and correct errors, and thus would inevitably find themselves involved with their employees and with government on another broad front. And overall the government (or private contractors paid by the government) would have to continually report on and update the status of millions of small individual IAs—a task that would

automatically result in the creation of a huge and potentially contro-
versial database of information on individuals' investments.

Only the government agencies involved are in a position to say
how all of these operational difficulties might be addressed. It seems
clear, however, that decisions about whether or not to advocate such
a plan should not be made solely on the basis of broad goals. The
agencies that would be held responsible for the successful operation
of the plan should have an opportunity to determine the feasibility of
doing the job before, not after, the political decision is made. There
would be little tolerance by the public for errors in administering a
plan in which each dollar deducted from earnings is seen as belong-
ing to a particular individual. And there is ample opportunity for
error in carrying out all the necessary tasks.

Perhaps most problematic for the administration in charge of implementing the plan would be the public's assessment of whether it is going
well. Headlines after three or four years of implementation to the effect
that millions of items cannot be assigned to any individual and that so
many hundreds of millions of dollars of deductions from workers' earnings cannot be identified and credited to IAs could cause serious political
repercussions—even though the government would not really be at fault,
since the problem would have originated with inaccurate reporting.[9]

An administration could suffer politically if the public perceived
that implementation of the plan was not going smoothly and fairly.
When just about every income-earning, tax-paying citizen is affected,
negative perceptions, whether accurate or not, can be detrimental to
public trust—and difficult to dispel, as the Postal Service and the
Internal Revenue Service can testify. And it doesn't take a lot of mistakes to create a bad impression. In the case of tax collection, many
Americans may not particularly value a high degree of accuracy, and
political leaders by and large would rather live with errors and lost
revenue than invite taxpayer unrest by deploying more IRS agents to
improve the accuracy of reporting. But administration of a savings
plan is something else. People will want to receive—and to be confident that they will *always* receive—full credit for their deductions
from earnings. Government better get this one right, and in advance.

Is the IA plan worth all the trouble? Comparing the plan with
the various combinations of proposals outlined in Chapter 2 points
up the fact that the IA plan relies on higher deductions from workers'
earnings to buy higher benefits for some participants (those with
above-average returns from investments) at the cost of lower benefits

for others, along with less certainty for all participants about which group they might end up in—the group that gets little more than the basic Social Security benefit (30 percent lower on average than under present law) or the group that gets more than under present law because of investments. In total, of course, the greater deductions buy higher benefits on a group basis (although the greater administrative costs of individual accounts need to be factored in). For individuals, however, the amount of retirement income will be uncertain, since so much depends on the movement of the stock market and the timing of one's entry into, and retirement from, the labor market.

5

CONCLUSION

Social Security policy should be conservative, in the sense of retaining what works best for most people. This argues for keeping Social Security as the basic part of a three-tier retirement system, maintained as a fully defined-benefit plan governed by the same nine major principles that have traditionally governed and still govern the program (see Appendix, The Nine Guiding Principles of Social Security). With the foundation of a multitier system secure, supplementary private pensions and savings investments may more reasonably take chances with the level of future benefits (although I believe that ordinarily the first part of a private pension system should also be a defined-benefit plan, with the riskier provision of 401(k)s and IRAs supplementary to that).

I see little reason to compromise on individual accounts. On the contrary, I believe that a public education campaign could build strong support for strengthening the present Social Security system by adopting alternatives that spread the cost of bringing the system into balance among current and future beneficiaries and present and future workers without imposing intolerable costs on anyone and without taking on the problems associated with individual accounts. And investing part of the accumulating Social Security funds in equities would make the task of achieving long-range balance relatively easy.

It is possible, of course, that no consensus will emerge from bipartisan consideration of possible Social Security changes. Even so, there could still be progress. If it had been their objective, a majority of the Advisory Council could quite easily have agreed on a plan that would have postponed trust fund exhaustion from about 2030 to 2050 and reduced the average deficit over the 75-year estimating period from 2.23 percent of payroll to 0.72 percent of payroll, a figure within "close actuarial balance." I would much prefer taking steps now to eliminate the full 75-year deficit and to put the program in a sustainable position for the even longer run, and I would hope we could all agree to pursue this goal. But if that degree of unanimity is presently unattainable, I believe that most Americans, once the trade-offs are understood, would prefer to take the really quite modest steps that are needed to bring the system into full balance over 50 years and "close actuarial balance" over 75 years—postponing for now the goal of arriving at exact balance over the full 75-year period—rather than drastically curtail Social Security to make room for privatization.

Appendix

The Nine Guiding Principles of Social Security: Where They Came From, What They Accomplish

In the midst of the Great Depression, the founders of today's Social Security system took the bold step of establishing a new institution that they expected to be slow-growing but permanent. They wanted to make a decent retirement attainable for millions of Americans who would otherwise become dependent on their families or on public assistance when they grew too old to work or could no longer find employment. They wanted to protect workers' dependents by providing insurance to make the death of a breadwinner financially manageable. They wanted to put an end to the poorhouse by distributing program income so as to provide at least a minimally adequate benefit for everyone regularly contributing. And, foreseeing the inevitability of change—including the eventual need to insure against other major risks, such as disability and illness—they sought to design an institution based on sustainable principles.

Accordingly, they took the long view. They gave major emphasis to estimating program income and expenses over a much longer period than was customarily done in other countries, and this is still true today. The time frame of 75 years that is now used for Social Security is much longer than that used in almost all other contexts, from foreign social insurance programs to federal budgeting. The point, then and now, was not to try to pretend that anyone could really know precisely what would be happening in 75 or even 25 years; the point was that the planners of Social Security, in making exceptionally long-term commitments, wanted always to be looking far enough ahead to anticipate necessary improvements and make needed changes in ample time to preserve the integrity of the program.

That approach has served well. The legislation of 1935 and 1939 created the basic design of Social Security, and all major legislation since then can be seen as building on that design: extending coverage to more and more workers, improving the level of protection, adding protection against loss of income from long-term and total disability, providing protection for the elderly and disabled against the increasingly unmanageable cost of medical care, protecting against the erosion of income by inflation, and abolishing all statutory differences in the treatment of men and women.

These and many other accomplishments and adjustments have taken place within a framework consisting of nine major principles. Social Security is *universal; an earned right; wage-related; contributory and self-financed; redistributive; not means-tested; wage-indexed; inflation-protected; and compulsory.* As with any framework, the stability of the entire structure depends on the contribution made by each part, so it is useful to review these principles and how they work together.

1. **Universal:** Social Security coverage has been gradually extended over the years to the point where 96 out of 100 jobs in paid employment are now covered, with more than 142 million working Americans making contributions in 1997. The goal of complete universality can be reached by gradually covering those remaining state and local government positions that are not now covered.

2. **Earned right:** Social Security is more than a statutory right; it is an *earned* right, with eligibility for benefits and the benefit rate based on an individual's past earnings. This principle sharply distinguishes Social Security from welfare and links the program, appropriately, to other earned rights such as wages, fringe benefits, and private pensions.

3. **Wage-related:** Social Security benefits are related to earnings, thus reinforcing the concept of benefits as an earned right and recognizing that there is a relationship between one's standard of living while working and the benefit level needed to achieve income security in retirement. Under Social Security, higher-paid earners get higher benefits; the lower-paid get more for what they pay in.

4. **Contributory and self-financed:** The fact that workers pay earmarked contributions from their wages into the system also reinforces the concept of an earned right and gives contributors a moral claim on future benefits above and beyond statutory obligations. And, unlike many foreign plans, Social Security is entirely financed by dedicated taxes, principally those deducted from workers' earnings matched by employers, with the self-employed paying comparable amounts. The entire cost of benefits plus administrative expenses (less than one percent of income) is met without support from general government revenues.

   This self-financing approach has several advantages. It helps protect the program against having to compete against other programs in the annual general federal budget—which is appropriate, because this is a uniquely long-term program. It imposes fiscal discipline, because the total earmarked income for Social Security must be sufficient to cover the entire cost of the program. And it guards against excessive liberalization: contributors oppose major benefit cuts because they have a right to benefits and are paying for them, but they also oppose excessive increases in benefits because they understand that every increase must be paid for by increased contributions. Thus a semi-automatic balance is achieved between wanting more protection versus not wanting to pay more for it.

5. **Redistributive:** One of Social Security's most important goals is to pay at least a minimally adequate benefit to workers who are regularly covered and contributing, regardless of how low-paid they may be. This is accomplished through a redistributional formula that pays comparatively higher benefits to lower-paid earners. The formula makes good sense. If the system paid back to low-wage workers only the benefit that they could be expected to pay for from their own wages, millions of retirees would end

up on welfare even though they had been paying into Social Security throughout their working lives. This would make the years of contributing to Social Security worse than pointless, since earnings deductions would have reduced their income throughout their working years without providing in retirement any income greater than what would be available from welfare. The redistributional formula solves this dilemma.

6. **Not means-tested:** In contrast to welfare, eligibility for Social Security is not determined by the beneficiary's current income and assets, nor is the amount of the benefit. This is a crucial principle. It is the absence of a means test that makes it possible for people to add to their savings and to establish private pension plans, secure in the knowledge that they will not then be penalized by having their Social Security benefits cut back as a result of having arranged for additional retirement income. The absence of a means test makes it possible for Social Security to provide a stable role in anchoring a multitier retirement system in which private pensions and personal savings can be built on top of Social Security's basic, defined protection.

7. **Wage-indexed:** Social Security is portable, following the worker from job to job, and the protection provided before retirement increases as wages rise. Benefits at the time of initial receipt are brought up to date with recent wages, reflecting improvements in productivity and thus in the general standard of living. Without this principle, Social Security would soon provide benefits that did not reflect previously attained levels of living.

8. **Inflation-protected:** Once they begin, Social Security benefits are protected against inflation by periodic Cost-of-Living Adjustments (COLAs) linked to the Consumer Price Index. Inflation protection is one of Social Security's greatest strengths, and one that distinguishes it from other (except federal) retirement plans: no private pension plan provides guaranteed protection against inflation, and inflation protection under state and local plans, where it exists at all, is capped. Without COLAs, the real value of Social Security benefits would steadily erode over time, as is the case with unadjusted private pension benefits. Although a provision for automatic adjustment

was not part of the original legislation, the importance of protecting benefits against inflation was recognized, and over the years the system was financed to allow for periodic adjustment to bring benefits up to date. But this updating was done only after a lag. Provision for automatic adjustment was added in 1972.

9. **Compulsory:** Social Security compels all of us to contribute to our own future security. A voluntary system simply would not work. Some of us would save scrupulously, some would save sporadically, and some would postpone the day of reckoning forever, leaving the community as a whole to pay through a much less desirable safety-net system. With a compulsory program, the problem of adverse selection—individuals deciding when and to what extent they want to participate, depending on whether their individual circumstances seem favorable—is avoided (as is the problem of obtaining adequate funding for a large safety-net program serving a constituency with limited political influence).

* * *

In the midst of the Great Depression it took courage to enact a system based on these principles. The Great Depression was a time of enormous and immediate needs, but Social Security was designed to be a slow-growing tree, one that could not provide much shelter in the near term. The point, however, was that, once grown, it would be strong enough to weather bad times as well as good.

A contributory retirement system takes a long time to develop, since by definition those who are already retired are not eligible for benefits. Fifteen years after the program was set up, only 21 percent of the elderly were receiving benefits, and it was not until the 1950s that politicians began to see much advantage in championing improvements in Social Security. And it was only in the 1960s, three decades after enactment, that Social Security began having a major impact, paying benefits that were high enough and universal enough to significantly reduce poverty among the elderly, the disabled, and the survivors of beneficiaries. After the amendments of 1972 further increased benefits substantially and provided for automatic inflation protection, Social Security fully assumed the role planned for it as the all-important base of a multitier retirement system in which private pensions and individual savings are added to Social Security's defined protection.

The importance of that role would be difficult to exaggerate: today, Social Security is the only organized retirement plan—the *only* assured source of retirement income—for at least half of the total workforce. And it is the base upon which all who are able to do so can build the supplementary protection of pensions and individual savings.

Social Security has become and continues to be the most popular and successful social program in America's history because its guiding principles enable it to work exactly as intended: as America's family protection plan.

NOTES

1

1. There are, in fact, separate trust funds for old-age and survivors insurance and for disability insurance, but for most purposes these programs are treated as one. The 1998 Trustees Report was issued at the end of April 1998, too late to be used in this publication. The changes from the 1997 report, however, are slight and have no material bearing on the analysis and conclusions presented here.

2. The drop in the ratio of workers to beneficiaries is a major reason why Social Security contribution rates have gradually risen from 1 percent at first to the present 6.2 percent, and why that is insufficient to fully support the system. It bears emphasizing, however, that the drop in the ratio has been anticipated. There are no surprises here. Estimates of the future course of this ratio in the *1997 Annual Report of the Board of Trustees of the Federal Old-Age and Survivors Insurance and Disability Insurance Trust Funds* (Washington, D.C.: Government Printing Office, 1997) (hereafter referred to as the *1997 Trustees Report*) are very close to the estimates used at the time of the landmark 1983 Amendments, which at the time showed the program in long-range balance. The deficit that has since appeared has to do entirely with other factors—such as changes in actuarial methods and in the use of new sources of data, along with changed assumptions about the future growth of real wages, the incidence of disability, and so on. The underlying phenomenon of a decreasing number of workers per retiree had been fully anticipated in the financing of the program.

3. This does not necessarily mean that the total costs of dependency will track the total number of dependents. For example, the public and family costs of educating children may or may not be less than the cost of providing medical care to the elderly. Moreover, even if per capita costs were the same, it would be politically difficult indeed to shift the family-borne cost of most of child-rearing to the social cost of most of caring for the elderly. But looked at on the scale of the economic capacity of society as a whole, there is clearly a major cost offset in the decline in the number of children per worker that parallels the increase in the number of the elderly.

2

1. *1997 Annual Report.* In Social Security, costs are usually calculated as a percent of payroll, since workers' earnings (payrolls) are the main source of financing. This way of discussing the capacity of the financing of the system to pay expected benefits avoids the complications that would attend using dollar figures to measure one set of benefits in one time period versus another set of benefits in a different time period.

2. Whether these changes are politically feasible at the present time is unclear. Four years ago, when the administration and the Congress agreed on a modest increase in taxation of benefits by making up to 85 percent of Social Security benefits subject to the income tax—a change affecting only higher-income beneficiaries—this action became the basis for attacks on incumbent Democrats in the 1994 elections. Although taxing benefits to the extent they exceed what the worker paid in is a change that warrants consideration on the merits, I suspect that it could be passed only with strong bipartisan support. And repeal of the special exemption might be attacked by opponents as singling out low-income people for a benefit cut, even though this change is equitable and restores the principle of equal treatment for taxpayers of the same income level. Again, bipartisan support would be necessary to get the vote.

3. *Report of the 1994–1996 Advisory Council on Social Security,* Volume I: Findings and Recommendations (Washington, D.C.: Government Printing Office, 1997), pp. 97–99.

4. There is no strong theoretical argument against this proposal, which when combined with other quite minimal changes would bring the system into exact balance over the entire 75-year estimating period. Whether it could attract sufficient support for enactment is another question. At one point the Carter administration proposed such a change, but because of

employer opposition it developed little support in Congress, and this could well be the fate of any such proposal today.

5. *Report of the 1994–1996 Advisory Council*, pp. 83–86 and 100–101 (discussion of Maintain Benefits plan).

6. Some critics argue that Congress might interfere with the principle of neutrality in investments. My view, however, is that a system of very broadly indexed investments would protect Congress against pressure to favor one corporate constituent over another, and that most members of Congress would welcome this protection.

7. The fund would build faster as a result of investing in stocks, but the additional national savings accruing from Social Security investment in stocks would be very considerably offset by other savers having to increase their holdings of government bonds as compared to investment in stocks. This offset would be less than 100 percent, however. In comparing Social Security investment in stocks to stock investments by individual accounts, it bears noting that, unlike the build-up in the Social Security fund, returns from stock fund investments by private investors would not be entirely saved but would be partly taken out of savings and spent.

8. This part of the proposal may strike a particularly responsive chord. A reduction in the level of Social Security taxes is welcomed by some policymakers as a progressive move, but whether it is or not depends on what is proposed as a substitute or whether, as in this instance, there is no substitute at all, thus forcing a benefit cut.

A proportional tax on wages would not be a fair way to raise money for general purposes. The Social Security tax is the same rate on wages that count toward benefits whether one has a high or low income. Although this, of course, means that the amount of taxes rises with wages up to the maximum wage counted for benefits, such a proportional tax is more burdensome on those with the lowest incomes. As a payment toward Social Security benefits that are heavily weighted in favor of the low-paid, however, it is fair. The total system of Social Security—contributions and benefits—is highly progressive, and the deduction from workers' earnings earmarked for Social Security strengthens the earned right to benefits in a way that no other method of financing can duplicate.

This is not to say that some general revenue subsidy for Social Security is out of the question, but it is to say that the major source of support should continue to come from deductions from workers' earnings and employer contributions that at least match those of their employees.

9. The Moynihan plan would affect more than Social Security. By making a 1 percent reduction in the Consumer Price Index—which governs both the Social Security cost-of-living adjustment and automatic changes in income tax brackets—it would, for example, very significantly increase income tax revenues.

3

1. In contrast, the IA plan discussed below would require an *immediate* increase of 1.6 percent of payroll, and the Personal Savings Account (PSA) plan recommended by five members of the 1994–96 Advisory Council calls for an immediate increase of approximately the same amount (1.52 percent of payroll).

2. Raising the possibility of moving the rate up could precipitate a debate about whether the program should instead adjust to any greater-than-expected growth in cost by cutting back on benefits. This argument might be avoided by providing that if the effective date is moved up by a specified number of years, half of the fail-safe adjustment would be in the form of a contribution-rate increase and the other half as a benefit cut.

If Social Security benefits are cut back now, thus trimming the prospective trust fund deficits, reduced spending by elderly recipients may slow the economy. That in turn would diminish any budgetary savings brought about by cutting Treasury outlays for Social Security. If a commitment were made now to make benefits less generous in the future, and if people now working took this into account—a big if—it might also reduce current spending, as those who could afford to do so would try to set aside more for their old age. If this did not slow the economy—again a big if— it might result in more aggregate saving and investment, thus contributing to future output and income in the economy as a whole.

4

1. Among the various privatization schemes currently in circulation the IA plan is examined here because it departs the least from the present system and thus seems to have the best chance of generating broad support. On the other hand, it produces such low supplementary benefits that rival privatizers quite reasonably question whether it is worth making such a wrenching change for such a small result.

2. These cuts result from: (1) changing the benefit formula; (2) raising the normal retirement age beyond the age sixty-five to age sixty-seven change scheduled in present law; and (3) increasing the number of years over which average wages are computed for benefit calculation purposes. Other plans, too, include one or more of these proposals.

3. IA proponents expect the government to offer workers a choice of investing in one or more of five to ten plans, some of which would be

indexed equity funds, some all-bond or all-government-securities funds, and some with mixed portfolios, with the government responsible for each fund's investments. It should be noted that any concerns about government investing directly in stocks, as discussed in Chapter 2, would apply equally to the IA plan.

4. It can be argued, however, that some getting less than average returns would still get more for what they pay even though getting lower benefits than now promised, because to restore the present program to long-term balance requires making changes to meet a 2.23 percent of payroll deficit, as compared to the 1.6 percent increase in deductions from workers' wages required by the IA plan.

5. Burtless's calculations are based on historical stock market prices and dividends from the Standard & Poor's Composite Stock Price Index dating back to 1872. Workers are assumed to have a career path of real earnings that matches the age-earnings profile of employed men in 1995. In addition, it is assumed that economy-wide wage growth is 2 percent per year after adjusting for inflation. Each worker is assumed to enter the work force on his 22d birthday and to work for 40 years until his 62d birthday. He saves 6 percent of his earnings and invests those savings exclusively in common stocks. All stock dividends are reinvested and are free of individual income taxes when received. Unlike ordinary investors, who must pay buying and selling costs when they trade stocks, the worker is assumed to face no transaction costs in making his investments.

On his 62d birthday, the worker converts his accumulation into a single-life annuity. The insurance company selling the annuity bases its charge on the expected mortality experience of American males reaching age 65 in 1995, using projections of the Social Security actuary. Unlike annuities actually available in today's marketplace, the insurance company does not charge a load factor to cover its profit requirements or possible adverse selection among people who wish to buy annuities. (Thus, the worker is assumed to buy a "fair" annuity.) In determining the sales price of the annuity, the insurance company assumes it will be able to invest the worker's funds at the six-month commercial paper interest rate prevailing when the annuity is purchased.

The figure shows the replacement rate for workers retiring in successive years from 1912 to 1997, with the replacement rate defined as the real value of the annuity divided by the worker's real average earnings when he was between 54 and 58 years old (that is, when he was earning his peak lifetime earnings). For example, the figure shows a replacement rate of 50 percent in 1912. This reflects the real value of the 1912 annuity available to a worker who began to work in January 1872, worked and saved for 40 years, and retired in January 1912. The replacement rate in 1942 was just 19 percent, while in 1997 it was 72 percent.

As this exercise demonstrates, replacement rates can vary enormously over relatively short periods of time. The replacement rate was 104 percent for workers retiring in 1969, but just 39 percent for workers retiring in 1975. Pensions depend crucially on when workers buy stocks and when they convert their nest eggs into annuities.

As pointed out in "Investing the Trust Fund in Equities," by Alicia H. Munnell and Pierluigi Balduzzi (Public Policy Institute, American Association of Retired Persons, March 1998), this variation in replacement rates (defined as the ratio of real annuity payment to real average wage at 54 to 58) reflects two major sources of uncertainty. The first is the performance of the stock market. Although real returns have been good during all the 40-year periods in the last 130 years, the difference between the high (9 percent) and low (4 percent) average return has important implications for the size of the nest egg to be annuitized under the IA plan. The second source of uncertainty is the nominal interest rate at the time of retirement. The higher the interest rate, the bigger the annuity payment. Thus people who enjoy high stock market returns and who retire when interest rates are high will have large retirement benefits relative to pre-retirement earnings, while those who face poorer stock market performance and retire when interest rates are low will end up with low replacement rates. In this illustration, pensions of workers who retired in 1970 would have been three times larger than those paid to workers who retired just seven years later. This variation does not result from picking the right stocks but is largely the result of the date of retirement. (An assumption that as they near retirement age investors gradually move part of their portfolio from stocks to bonds would make the changes in the graph less abrupt, but the retirement date would still be of prime importance in determining benefit levels.)

6. *Fixing Social Security: A Statement by the Research and Policy Committee of the Committee for Economic Development.* Critique by Josh S. Weston, chairman of the Research and Policy Committee, with which committee member Peter A. Benoliel asked to be associated (Committee for Economic Development, Washington, D.C., 1997). The CED plan would be more administratively difficult than the IA plan because there would be many more funds involved and they would be private funds, but many of the necessary administrative tasks would be the same.

7. The self-employed present a special difficulty in a compulsory savings plan, in part because of their ability to manipulate any requirements to their own advantage, but presumably they would have to be covered, since the IA plan necessarily cuts their Social Security benefits along with those of employees.

8. The more sweeping privatization plans such as the PSA plan would involve still greater administrative difficulty because employees would be allowed to put their money into just about any generally available investment

vehicle, choosing multiple vehicles if they wish. Employers would have to play a major role in administering these plans, explaining the system and choices to employees and getting the required deductions to the right place for prompt investment. It would be very difficult for the government, having required employers to make these deductions, to follow through and make sure the money is received by one or several employee-designated agents for investment, following the allocation changes as employees direct, seeing that the full amount deducted plus earnings is held to retirement with total investments and earnings reported back to the employees and required corrections made of alleged reporting errors as identified by employees.

It can be argued that some employers now do much of this administrative work for 401(k) plans. But the situations are quite different. Employers have a strong incentive to make voluntary salary-reduction defined-contribution plans such as 401(k)s attractive to their employees since such plans are much less costly for employers than defined-benefit pension plans. Thus employers—mostly quite large employers—offering 401(k)s are motivated to keep employees satisfied with their 401(k) choices, and regard the associated expenses of education and reporting as cost-effective investments. In contrast, a government-required plan covering employers without 401(k) plans may well be viewed by them solely as an added burden and cost, and efforts by government to assure compliance with the rules are likely to be seen as another regulatory nuisance. There is real doubt that such wide-choice plans could be adequately supervised by government at manageable cost.

9. A cautionary historical note: In the early days of Social Security, inability to credit to individual accounts what seemed in the aggregate to be a very large number of wage items (although few would have significantly affected benefit amounts) prompted critical headlines for a long period of time, creating a significant and persistent public relations problem.

INDEX

ABOUT THE AUTHORS

Robert M. Ball was commissioner of Social Security from 1962 to 1973, serving under Presidents Kennedy, Johnson, and Nixon. He was a member of the 1982–83 National Commission on Social Security Reform (the Greenspan Commission), a visiting scholar at the Center for the Study of Social Policy, and senior scholar at the Institute for Medicine. His numerous publications include *Pensions in the United States*; *Social Security: Today and Tomorrow*; and *Because We're All in This Together* (on long-term care). He contributed the concluding chapter to *Social Security in the 21st Century*, edited by Eric R. Kingson and James H. Schulz (New York: Oxford University Press, 1997). He was a member of the 1989–91 and 1994–96 Advisory Councils on Social Security and has served on many other advisory groups. A founding member of the National Academy of Social Insurance, he chaired its board of directors from 1986–1996.

Thomas N. Bethell is a Washington, D.C., writer and editor who has produced numerous reports on policy issues ranging from occupational safety and rural economic development to health care and the future of Social Security. He has previously worked with Robert M. Ball on *Because We're All in This Together*, *Social Security in the 21st Century*, the final report of the 1994–96 Advisory Council on Social Security, and other reports.